Alan Hall

Series Editor:
Terry Marsh

DALESMAN

Dalesman Publishing Company
Stable Courtyard, Broughton Hall,
Skipton, North Yorkshire BD23 3AE

First Edition 1996
© Alan Hall 1996

A British Library Cataloguing in Publication record
is available for this book

ISBN 1 85568 105 6

Other books in this series:
South Pennines by John Gillham
(ISBN 1 85568 106 4)

The information given in this book has been provided in good
faith and is intended only as a general guide. Whilst all
reasonable efforts have been made to ensure that details were
correct at the time of publication, the author and Dalesman
Publishing Company Ltd cannot accept any responsibility for
inaccuracies. It is the responsibility of individuals undertaking
outdoor activities to approach the activity with caution and,
especially if inexperienced, to do so under appropriate
supervision. They should also carry, and be capable of using
properly, the appropriate equipment and maps, be properly
clothed and have adequate footwear. The sport described in this
book is strenuous and individuals should ensure that they are
suitably fit before embarking upon it.

Contents

INTRODUCTION

"horas non numero nisi serenas" – *I number none but shining hours.*

THE APPEAL OF THE NORTH PENNINES
First visual impressions of this compact upland area, unknown by many, unwalked by most, are of a table-top of severe, wilderness moorlands, fine of form, as moorlands go, but somewhat lacking in eye appeal. Subsequent and closer, indeed intimate, feet-on experience exposes the pedestrian to an incurable addiction to further exploration, revealing that, as usual, first impressions can be misleading.

Covering approximately 940 square miles/2600 square kilometres between the A66, the A68, the A69 and the River Eden, these brooding fells comprise innumerable interlinked heather- and grass-clad moors and dividing dales. Lonely places, scattered with the skeletons of yesterday, that were and still are influenced by the all-pervading triumvirate of Cross Fell, John Wesley and lead. The broad bulk of Cross Fell, at 2,930ft/893m the highest mountain in the North (indeed, the whole) Pennines, and its surrounding supplicants, exert an influence on climate and all living things that far exceeds their equivalent in other ranges. Cross Fell dominates the North Pennines, as did the mining of lead and the lead miner, and John Wesley, the father of Methodism. No matter where in the North Pennines, the influence of one, or all, can be seen or experienced.

These endless fells and probing dales present a divergence of geological architecture, embroidered by the visible evidence of man's presence and passage throughout the centuries. Couple that with unequalled solitude, and the scenically pleasing and diverse packaging of the area, and it presents an inviting and challenging parcel waiting to be opened by walkers of all persuasions.

From East Fellside to the green and bountiful vales and dales of Eden, Lunedale, Baldersdale, Teesdale, Weardale, Derwentdale, Allendale, South Tynedale and Nentdale, there is more to find than peat and worked out seams of galena. Indeed, for walkers who wish to see and to find, there lies in these hills and dales a veritable cornucopia.

Unlike many of the saturated honeypots, the North Pennines offer the walker space, and, in certain sectors, total wilderness solitude. They personify all that is best in fell and dale, crag and scar and miners' ways, plus a spread of indigenous wildlife that is second to none.

For clarity, and ease of use, the guide divides the North Pennines into eight sections. Each section, with the exception of the first, contains a dale, or two if they are small, with from two to nine typical walks, dependent on the size of the dale. The first section contains "tasters", that is, walks on the outer fringes, that are not only fine walks in their own right, but also provide revealing and tempting sightings of the North Pennines.

Subsequently, the sections progress through the North Pennines in a clockwise direction, starting with West and East Allendale, Derwentdale, Weardale, Teesdale, Baldersdale and Lunedale, Eden Vale and East Fellside, and concluding with South Tynedale and Nentdale.

Each differs in character, as will be seen, yet all are bound by that invisible, unbreakable thread of quiet strength that is their North Pennine heritage.

For the gentle rambler and the initiate, the lower dales present a tempting picture of pastoral peace and intriguing waterways, richly endowed with flora and fauna of a unique nature. Indeed, the Teesdale Assemblage enjoys an international reputation. History, social and industrial, abounds, as do tales and legends of local happenings and characters. All combine to ensure that North Pennine walks, however short or gentle, will stimulate and encourage the participant to explore just that little bit further the next time. The walks included in the guide are intended to demonstrate the wide range that is available.

Another plus is the unique scenic appeal of wild fell and thunderous water, often enhanced by visible reminders of physical and social history. Such assets and their inherited tracks and ways more than compensate for the lack of naked rock or Munro heights, by providing pleasing routes along which the pedestrian can walk with eager anticipation, and not a little aplomb.

Challenge, however, is also present, for on the exposed high fells and ridges glutinous peat is not unknown, nor are the arctic winds that pulse in from distant Siberia to produce a home-grown fiend, the Helm Wind. Such hazards make the heights of East Fellside, upper Teesdale and upper Weardale a destination for the well prepared and experienced.

ACCESS
Road links:
Unlike so many of Britain's upland playgrounds, the North Pennines have motorways, trunk roads and A-roads that provide easy access to the perimeter, from where further A-roads encircle the high ground. However, only the A689 Alston to Wolsingham, the B6276 Brough to Middleton, the B6277 Alston and Teesdale, the B6278 Barnard Castle to Edmundbyers, and the B6295 Allendale Town to Weardale roads bisect the fells, and can claim direct contact with the exposed interior.

Several unclassified ribbons of Tarmac tentatively probe the dales, though few emerge successfully at the other side.

Rail links:
Two InterCity main lines pass by the perimeter of the North Pennines, stopping at Penrith and Carlisle on the west coast line, and Darlington, Durham and Newcastle on the east coast link. Local lines connect Newcastle to Carlisle and West Yorkshire to Settle, from where the scenic Settle to Carlisle service can be enjoyed. This regional railway connects with local bus services into the North Pennines at Langwathby, and also offers a selection of guided walks from the line.

Bus services:
Long distance express bus services from major cities and towns in England and Scotland pass by the fringes of the North Pennines, stopping at Darlington, Newcastle, Penrith and Carlisle.

Local services:
For an area publicised as the "Last Wilderness", it is remarkably well served by local buses. No less than thirteen operators, including a Royal Mail post bus, provide transport into and through the North Pennines. Between them they connect Allendale Town, Allenheads, Alston, Appleby-in-Westmorland, Barnard Castle, Blanchland, Brampton, Brough, Carlisle, Castleside, Cowshill, Crook, Darlington, Durham, Edmundbyers, Haltwhistle, Haydon Bridge, Hexham, Ireshopeburn, Langwathby, Melmerby, Middleton-in-Teesdale, Nenthead, Newcastle, Rookhope, St. John's Chapel, Stanhope and Wolsingham.

Hadrian's Wall also has its own regular bus service, operating from Hexham and Carlisle.

Free copies of a collective Bus and Train Services – Across the Roof of England *timetable, are available throughout the area covered by this guide.*

Access on foot
There are acres of space, and many miles of public paths, bridleways and permissive paths running through a designated Area of Outstanding Natural Beauty (AONB), administered by the councils of Northumberland, Cumbria and Durham. The North Pennines' AONB does not include all of Teesdale, Weardale, Hamsterley Forest and Slaley Forest.

Many public rights of way utilise old Roman roads, drove roads, trade roads, carriers' ways, mine tracks and paths from village to farm, mine or church. Extensive though the network is, there are invariably blanks on the map, preventing access to the desired goal ahead. There are also, in the AONB, "no-go" areas. Some are seasonal, such as those involved in the annual hatching and dispatching of grouse. Others, like the MOD Warcop Firing Ranges are, to all practical intents and purposes, total. Fortunately, they are situated on land that has little, if any, appeal to the hill walker, being invariably covered in trackless tangled heather and black hag, with little that pleases the eye. And, in the case of the MOD ranges, peppered with unexploded devices.

Limited restrictions, for understandable reasons, are imposed in the National Nature Reserves, Sites of Special Scientific Interest and the RSPB Reserve.

Considerate and careful walkers will appreciate that the great majority of walks in the guide utilise waymarked public paths and bridleways, country lanes, permissive paths and old rail tracks. If in doubt, please verify the route with the OS 1:25 000 Outdoor Leisure map.

Concerning the few parts of walks not shown as public paths on the map, approval to include the route has been obtained from the farmer, (Walk 23), or Forest Enterprise (Walks 2, 17, 25 and 26). In the case of Walk 22, the section along two county boundaries has been hallowed by custom and tradition, and is also included in previous guides.

Accommodation:
There is a wide range of overnight stays to suit all tastes, including eight youth hostels and four camping barns. The youth hostels are at Baldersdale, Dufton, Langdon Beck, Alston, Edmundbyers, Ninebanks, Greenhead and Once Brewed. Six are on the Pennine Way, making it advisable to book in advance during the summer months. Camping barns, a recent innovation in the North Pennines, are situated at Wearhead, Holwick, Lartington and Witton.

NORTH PENNINE WALKING
It is not the intention of this guide to lead the reader by the hand, for that will blunt the sharp edge of discovery and achievement. Is it not more rewarding and satisfying for the walker to be pointed in the right direction and informed what to expect along the way?

There is a mixed selection of forty-three walks, from low-level strolls to high and hard hikes, with the majority slotting somewhere between the two.

Each walk has its own character, symbolising the surrounds, and is full of items of interest along the way. Be not deterred by hearsay, or perhaps first impressions; choose a clear day with a good companion and enjoy the North Pennines.

Underfoot
Some of the short low-level walks are so benign, in places,

that trainers can be worn. The majority, however, require stout footwear as they traverse pasture and riverside paths, stony miners' tracks and, occasionally, boulderfields or peaty open fell. Sections can be very wet underfoot in winter or after long periods of rain.

Equipment
The choice is effective and simple – clothes to keep you cool and comfortable in summer, dry and warm in winter, not forgetting that the heights of the North Pennines can be cold and inhospitable, while the dale's floor may be comfortably warm. For any day on the fells always carry map and compass (with the ability to use both), water, a high energy snack, first aid kit, torch and whistle.

Maps
Excellent Ordnance Survey® maps cover the whole of the North Pennines. For the walks contained in this book, you will need one or more of the following:

Outdoor Leisure Map:
Sheet 31: North Pennines: Teesdale and Weardale

Landranger Sheets:
86: Haltwhistle, Bewcastle and Alston area
87: Hexham, Haltwhistle and surrounding area
88: Tyneside and Durham area
90: Penrith, Keswick and Ambleside area
91: Appleby-in-Westmorland
92: Barnard Castle and surrounding area

Pathfinder Sheet:
570: Allenheads and Rookhope

Safety
Always inform someone of your intentions, route and esti-mated time of return (ETR), but if that is not possible,

leave the information in a conspicuous place in your car. Some walkers are reluctant to leave such information within sight in the car due to the increase in car crime, but it is a risk worth taking. Cars and their radios can be replaced; a life sacrificed by a twelve-hour delay cannot.

Simple rules apply should injury occur: a basic knowledge of first aid, familiarity with the rescue procedures (Tel: 999 Police, for the Mountain Search and Rescue Team, giving details of the injury and position).

LONG-DISTANCE WALKS
The two main dales, Weardale and Teesdale, offer waymarked ways, each basically following its river from the North Sea to the dale's head, although for the initial days the route is not through the North Pennines as such. The eight youth hostels and four camping barns in the area can be linked, providing a long-distance route of your choosing, although much of the southern half may have to be on the Pennine Way.

Two national long-distance walks, the Pennine Way and the Alternative Pennine Way, pass through, each spending five to seven days in the area, and each in its way examining in depth the varying character of the North Pennines. All the long-distance routes have much to commend them.

THE WEARDALE WAY:
The final 35 miles, above Wolsingham to the Killhope Wheel-Allenheads loop, probes most corners of Weardale's floor. At times, between Eastgate and Westgate and by Killhope and Allenheads, it offers a taste of the high fells.

THE TEESDALE WAY:
Similar in design to the Weardale Way, as far as its entry into the North Pennines by Paradise Walk to Barnard

Castle. From here it enters a dale of pleasing villages, pastures and riverside walks that contain two of the most breathtaking waterfalls in England.

HOSTEL & CAMPING BARN LINKS:
Such is the network of twelve budget overnight sites, it allows the independent walker to choose and plan a route of exploration, by utilising the many public pathways that criss-cross the North Pennines.

THE ALTERNATIVE PENNINE WAY:
Assuming entry is made from Appleby-in-Westmorland to Dufton, although there is no reason not to enter from Hadrian's Wall, the route then samples the old Dufton-Nenthead lead road, over Great Dun Fell to the South Tyne and onward to Nenthead. The Way provides extensive views and much of interest about the lead mining days. An airy way then leads to yesterday's klondyke of Allendale Town, prior to a scenic passage through two dales to Haltwhistle in South Tynedale, and beyond to Hadrian's Wall. A total of 47 miles/75.2km in the North Pennines.

THE PENNINE WAY:
By contrast, the Pennine Way walks through 68 miles/ 108.8km of the North Pennines, sampling both extremes of the scenic spectrum. Entry, over the A66(T) on to Bowes Moor can, in poor weather, dampen the spirits. However, as the glistening waters of Baldersdale and Lunedale are passed and Teesdale entered, the step will quicken, for ahead lies the River Tees, Low Force, High Force, Cronkley Fell, Falcon Clints, Cauldron Snout, Cow Green, High Cup Gill and Dufton; perhaps the most stimulating and scenic stretch of the entire Pennine Way.

NORTH PENNINE COUNTRY CODE

PROTECT plants, trees and wildlife

GUARD against all risk of fire

KEEP dogs and domestic animals under control

LEAVE dogs at home during lambing and nesting times (April to mid-June)

OBSERVE – not INSPECT – old mine workings

OBSERVE all signs - do not leave open or obstruct gates

AVOID damaging walls, fences, hedges, signs and buildings

RESPECT others' property and the work of the countryside

CONTRIBUTE to the peace and quiet of the North Pennines

Location Map

The numbers on this location map roughly indicate the starting point of each of the walks in the book.

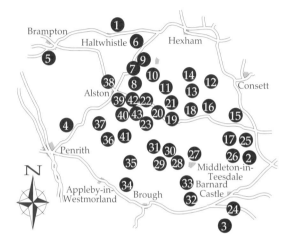

OUTSIDE LOOKING IN

To examine what the North Pennines have to offer the walker before boots are laced, five walks are suggested on the fringes of the area. Not only do they provide sightings of the North Pennines in a variety of guises and moods, but in their own right they are walks of style and interest, to suit all abilities and tastes. Each of the five, positioned at different points around the area, allows a wide range of sightings, and at the same time varies the character and challenge of the walks themselves.

The first of these "taster" walks embraces the highest point on Hadrian's Wall, on the Whin Sill crags north of the A69(T). It is a journey that allows fine views of the north-west fells and the great sweep of South Tynedale.

Then, Hamsterley Forest, a balanced mix of conifers and broadleaves, south of Wolsingham and the A689, provides an abundance of pleasing walks, and is the venue of the easterly window looking out over the dividing fells of Weardale and Teesdale. To the south-east, fringing the Yorkshire boundary, rise How Tallon and The Stang, both fine grandstands from which to look deep into Teesdale, and beyond, to the outer rim of Weardale.

The final two walks stroll through the Vale of Eden, one close to Langwathby; the other to Brampton and the A69(T), to gaze on the escarpments and rounded summits of East Fellside, while treading ancient ways by a druid's circle and a mysterious tarn.

1 Hadrian's Wall

For approximately 6 miles/9.6km the walk journeys alongside the Wall, and includes the fort of Vercovicium (Housesteads), providing extensive views of the North Pennines, including South Tynedale, to the south. The remaining miles cover the crags, fells and lough-sides north of the wall. This journey through time, although passing information boards along the way, is enhanced by further study.

Distance:
14 1/4 miles/23.6km

Height gain:
1,099ft/335m

Walking time:
7 hours

Start/Finish:
Once Brewed Visitor Centre and Youth Hostel. GR753669: 4 miles/6.4km north-east from Haltwhistle and 6 miles/9.6km east from Greenhead. Car park and facilities.

Type of walk:
A long circular walk, with frequent bursts of ascent and descent. It includes grass paths and stony ways, pasture crossings, cart tracks, country lanes and the Pennine Way.

The Northumberland National Park Visitor Centre at Once Brewed provides not only a convenient start, but also a wealth of information about the Wall.

The Wall was built following Hadrian's visit to Britain in AD122, and was planned as a continuous barrier of stone or earth, with defensive ditches. It stretched for 80 Roman miles, i.e. 75 miles/120km, from coast to coast, the most effective defensive line in the Roman Empire.

Cross the busy B6318 Military Road, with care, to walk north for 800yds/m to the Wall, passing the tidy Peel Bothy on the right prior to a fingerpost (Winshields Crag ³/₄ mile), pointing west. Continue with the road to the ridge top, i.e. the Wall itself, to turn left over a stone stile, with a waymark (Shield on the Wall 1³/₄ miles). As height is gained, the Wall and its visible foundations are revealed. With the approach of the trig pillar on Windshields Crag, higher examples of the Wall appear.

Windshields Crag, the highest point on the Wall, is strategically placed between Housesteads Fort and Milecastle 42, allowing stunning views both near and far. There are good views of the north-facing dolerite crags along which the Wall was built, and distant sweeps of Northumbria's fells, plus the solid rise south of the North Pennines.

On the descent to Caw Gap there are variations, of restored Wall, not-so-restored Wall and vandalised Wall. Caw Gap by Shield on the Wall demonstrates the ups and downs on Hadrian's Wall – steep and sharp. Cross the road and rise beside a stretch of restored Wall.

Caw Gap Turret 41A is one of many stone watch towers. There were two between each milecastle, built when the foundations of the Wall were laid, then linked to the Wall

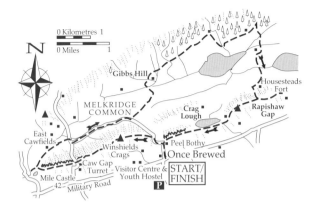

as it was constructed. By the end of the 2nd century AD the turret was out of use. Note the Wall's north ditch and the embankments and ditches of the Vallum to the south.

The walk over Cawfields Crags to Milecastle 42 displays sections of restored Wall that is two metres thick. Is there any significance in this width of two metres, for this is the width of the Roman Dere Street and the Maiden Way? Inspect the milecastle, with its information board, before passing through a gate and swinging right on to a farm track leading north-north-east by Cawfields Farm to East Cawfields Farm.

Small gated castles like Milecastle 42, positioned every Roman mile (1.48km) along the Wall, housed the troops who manned and maintained the Wall, in addition to controlling the flow of barbarians from the north. As the Latin quotation says "qui barbaros Romanosque divideret" – "to divide the Romans from the barbarians". The building of the entire Wall was under the direction of Aulus Platorius Nepos, the Roman Governor of Britain, on orders directly from Emperor Publius Aelius Hadrianus.

Just prior to East Cawfields Farm, a public path leads half right (north-east) through fell pastures for 800yds/m, to a quiet north/south country lane. Turn right on to the lane, then left at the junction, to stride east over Melkridge Common for 1¼ miles/2km. With Sook Hill, Well House and Saughy Rigg to the north and the Wall-bearing crags to the south, the junction of Gibbs Hill is soon reached.

Descend left (north-east) over the cattle grid, into the green and gently-folding valley of Caw Burn, north below Hound Hill. As if to compensate for the loss of the Wall crags, the dramatic profile of Sewingshields Crags fills the eastern skyline beyond Housesteads. Take the left fork for Gibbs Hill, then loop left with the public footpath sign on a stone track to cross Gibbshill Fell north-east. Please keep to the waymarked tracks, and close all gates, as the signpost (East Stonefolds 2½ miles) is followed to the blanket of sitka spruce ahead.

More waymarked stiles and a good track aid progress north-east, alongside the endless conifers, to the farm of Greenlee. Swing right through the waymarked steading for a short walk south, with a jutting forest spur, before turning left on to a grass path by Old Stonefolds. Here the public path passes the front door and the garden (no objections from the occupier) as it continues to East Stonefolds.

What a daunting prospect the Wall-topped crags must have presented to any cattle-grabbing Picts who ventured south from the dark lands. Nineteen centuries ago it would have been an impassable wilderness.

As the track descends east from East Stonefolds turn

right (south) with the Pennine Way and cross, by a stile, into dull and damp moorland. Beyond the remains of Cragend ascend south on improving grass tracks to the V of Rapishaw Gap between Cuddy's Crags and Hotbank Crags. The left turn to Housesteads Fort injects extra distance to the circuit, and entry is not free, but do not miss the opportunity. The routes are well-signposted.

Housesteads, originally Borcovicium and later Vercovicium, is the finest remaining example of a Roman fort or garrison (it held 1,000 troops) in Europe. Wall forts were placed at intervals of approximately 13 miles/20.8km, or 14 Roman miles, i.e. a day's march apart.

Return to Rapishaw Gap and ascend Hotbank Crags west with the Wall, for a stimulating journey on what is perhaps the most dramatically scenic section of the 74 mile/118.3km Hadrian's Wall. Pass along the way, keeping to the Wall, not the military track, passing in turn Hotbank Farm, the dark pearl of Crag Lough below Highshield Crag, the sharp stony drop of Castle Nick by Milecastle 39, and Peel Crags. Take care above Crag Lough once clear of the trees, as the unfenced edge of Highshield Crag encroaches on to the footpath. From the sloping west end of Peel Crags, it is just a short walk to the lone building of Peel Bothy and the returning road south to Once Brewed on the B6318.

2 Hamsterley Forest

A journey for the family, that goes just a little bit further into the depths of this inviting forest. Interest along the waymarked way is high, passing the site of an illicit whisky still and a part-finished millstone, in the constant company of a variety of forest wildlife.

Distance:
4½ miles/7.2km

Height gain:
597ft/182m

Walking time:
2½ hours

Start/Finish:
Hamsterley Forest, The Grove Car Park. GR066298: signposted, via minor roads, 3½ miles/5.6km west from Hamsterley and 7 miles/11.2km south of Wolsingham.

Type of walk:
A pleasant circular forest walk, on forest roads and stony tracks, never severe or claustrophobic, although after long periods of rain, conditions underfoot can be muddy.

A nominal toll is charged for the Forest Drive and car parks.

The secluded Grove Car Park provides an ideal setting for the starting point. One-time "shooting residence" of the

Surtees family, whose Bedburn estate was bought by the Forestry Commission, The Grove was described in 1885 by W. Herbert Smith in Weardale Walks as "snugly ensconced in the bottom of a deep valley surrounded on all sides by steep acclivities, and embowered in woods." The only drawback being "the insatiable myriads of midges whose blood-sucking powers and propensities are intolerable." And so it remains today, although modern science has now given us the repellent Diethyltoluamide – "Diet" for short.

From the car park walk north-west with the green arrows of the Tree Trail, to meet a wide forest road. Turn left on to the road and over the crossroads, gradually ascending west for 800yds/m, above Strawberry Bank, to a junction coming in from the left. Turn left on to this winding track known in forestry circles, doubtless with some irony, as the Silver Mile, so named to link it with its neighbour, the Golden Mile. Both were costly constructions due to the road stone persistently sinking into the underlying peat. Bog-hoppers will no doubt sympathise.

Continue south-west for 1$^1/_2$ miles/2km with the Silver Mile, a contouring way flanked by a fine mix of colourful broadleaves high above Oak Bank and Spurlswood Beck. As the track swings right by a left-hand junction, note the cherry trees on the left, where a parasitic rowan is growing out of a rotting branch. Beyond the bend leave the track temporarily to plunge left into the conifers via an arrowed path winding through the steep-sided gully of Whisky Gill; a path that runs around the head of the small valley, passing two embryo millstones, before rejoining the forest road.

Whisky Gill marks the site of an illicit whisky still,

possibly constructed by a disillusioned Highland-man returning north from Bonnie Prince Charlie's unsuccessful '45 foray. The two partially-completed millstones appear to have been abandoned due to cracks or faults appearing during bedrock separation.

Once on the road, continue south for approximately 600yds/m to the angled junction, where a sharp left descent doubles back via a rough track and drops into Blackling Hole Car Park.

The present name of this picturesque linn cascading into a deep pool in Spurlswood Beck, seen beneath the car park bridge, is perhaps a misspelling or mispronunciation of the original name Black Linn. "Linn" is the Cymric or Celtic word denoting "the pool below the falls".

With some reluctance, for Spurlswood Beck has great appeal, the valley floor is left behind by ascending north-east with a Tarmac lane. At the fork, branch left with a grassy track that eventually crosses Greenless Beck to veer left again, heading north by the forest boundary. After 800yds/m of open ground on the right, re-enter the conifers once more at a crook in the perimeter fence. Join a forest path running north, above the valley floor, for 3/4 mile/1.2km before descending left, at a multi-junction, on to the road returning to The Grove.

This final leg offers fine sightings of Spurlswood Beck's tree-clad west bank, above which runs the Silver Mile of the outward route. Particularly outstanding is the mixture of old beech and oak with European larch growing on Oak Bank.

Hamsterley Forest, the largest forest in the North Pennines, was acquired by the Forestry Commission and planting

commenced in 1927. Today, it covers some 4,400 acres/2,000 hectares with over 60 different species, conifers in the main, but this forest is by no means a collection of monocultural blocks. Sites of scenic attraction, plus public and wildlife interest are planned to expand. By increasing areas of open space and broadleaf planting surrounding forest blocks, such improvements are mainly concentrated along watercourses, enabling them to act as wildlife corridors, in addition to diversifying the landscape. Annual production at present is in the region of 20,000 metric tonnes of timber.

3 The Stang and How Tallon

This circular adventure with the cheery company of moorland birds, offers not only three distinct ecocultures, but also an invitation to sample the far-ranging view of the south-eastern fastness of the North Pennines.

Distance:
10½ miles/16.8km

Height gain:
910ft/275m

Walking time:
5 hours

Start/Finish:
Barningham.
GR084102:
2 miles/3.2km south of
the A66 at Greta
Bridge. Limited
parking on the village
green and the long
street.

Type of walk:
A moderate circular
walk, with some
indistinct fell paths, but
generally along quiet
lanes, farm and forest
tracks, and grassy
heather-ways.

**Not recommended in
poor visibility.**

**Please do not block
residents' access.**

Barningham, is a rural delight, and provides the perfect platform from which to start this walk.

Stroll north-east down the village road, with the green

on the right, to pass the Milbank Arms before swinging sharp left at a farm. With the church towering on the left and pastures green to the right begin this anti-clockwise journey, known to Barningham folk as "Around the World".

First on a narrow lane that crosses the road to the Greta Bridge road and then following a farm track westwards, the walk continues along Low Lane and Cowclose Lane, via ford or footbridge and crumbling kiln, to rise with a mix of trees to join a country road. Turn left along this twisting lane for 600yds/m, as if returning to Barningham. At a cattle grid and gated lane, opposite a gravelled lay-by (which can be used as an alternative start and finish), turn right on to a farm track snaking south-west over open pastures. (Note and observe the nearby Barningham and Holgate Estates notice.)

For the next 3¹/₂ miles/5.6km the route treads Hope Road, a packhorse trail of centuries past, and provides a pleasing prospect with Barningham Moor rolling ever higher on the left and fingers of probing broadleaves enhancing the dyked pastures on the right. Pass, with gated way, the sturdy steadings of Bragg House, Moorcock and Haythwaite before swinging west to cross Woodclose Gill and enter, at a gate and notice board, the eastern fringes of Stang Forest. Soon the track bursts beyond the trees to pass by the solid stones of Far East Hope Farm and East Hope.

Take time to study the stones of the former: on the east gable a dressed strip below the apex bears the inscription "Glory to God 1796 in the Highest", and the stone window lintels left of the front door carry the words "Cheese Room" on the first floor, and "Dairy" on the ground floor.

Back with the trees, the now Tarmac lane provides fine views ahead of Spanham, perched on the skyline, before meeting a crossroads, at which the walk turns sharp left through a wicket gate on to a dirt and grass forest track. Although sitka-saturated, the mile of forest is never claustrophobic as the track heads southeast to join a wide forest road, that continues to the corner of East Hope's stone-dyked in-bye pastures before swinging east-south-east. Prior to Hope Edge and Woodclose Gill take a right fork to leave the main forest road and rise on a grass track to a forest boundary gate. Ahead lie the bleak heather and grass acres of Barningham Moor and High Band.

For the next stretch the paths are initially elusive, although shown on maps as public paths. Leave the trees, and cross Woodclose Gill heading south-east to higher ground. As the way ascends, swing slightly left on to a small ridge east-south-east, keeping the outcrops and Cross Gill on the left and the dome of High Band to the right. Once above the source of Osmaril Gill, with its interesting outcrops, loop southeast and south to meet the gated boundary wall of Durham and North Yorkshire. Follow the narrow path left to the trig pillar and domed summit of How Tallon.

On a clear day this vantage point (1,467ft/447m) will whet any walker's appetite as the moors and fells of Cotherstone, Stainmore, Teesdale and Weardale beckon and entice for the next 3 miles/4.8km.

The final leg of the walk, unhindered by navigation problems (being guided by the county boundary wall), allows a full appreciation of the views ahead. Though wet in places, the moor can be traversed with panache and anticipation, passing on the way two marker posts said to relate to Badger Way Stoop.

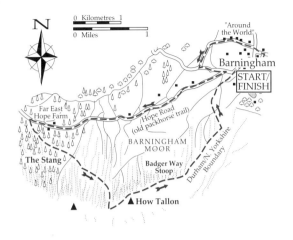

Badger Way Stoop is an old green road over Barningham Moor leading to Marske, and is named after the "badgers" – men who led strings of packhorses over the high moors. The first marker post, just north of the outcrops on the north face of How Tallon, is dressed in an unusual five-sided pattern and is inscribed, although now faint, as marking the Badger Way Stoop. The second nestles in the angle of the wall some 800yds/m north-east. Neither is on the line of Badger Way, which travels west on lower ground from the small col below Byers Hill.

At the old rail-wagon, by a gate into Yorkshire, leave the wall and swing left with a distinct cart track, descending north-north-west and north through tousy heather to pass the site of the Wemmergill Monument. A way that crosses gate and grid on to the roadway leads south into Barningham to conclude the walk.

4 Long Meg

In addition to the intriguing stone circle of Long Meg and her Daughters and the five rooms in Lacy's Caves, the walk also provides tempting sightings of East Fellside, including the massif of Cross Fell and the Pikes of Murton, Dufton and Knock to the east and south-east.

Distance:
7 miles/11.2km

Height gain:
148ft/45m

Walking time:
3 1/2 hours

Start/Finish:
Little Salkeld. GR566362: 1 3/4 miles/2.8km north of Langwathby and 6 1/2 miles/10.4km north-east from Penrith. Limited verge-side parking in the village.

Type of walk:
A circular walk of medium length, with many items of interest along the way. The route travels along country lanes plus well waymarked woodland and field paths.

Please do not obstruct access.

Little Salkeld, its Norse name means "a spring in the willows", with its fortified church, sets the scene for this eventful walk.

From the village green walk east, on the road signposted "Long Meg, Druid's Circle", to rise between high hedges and green pastures. Ahead, the first sightings of East Fellside, from Melmerby Fell over Cross Fell to Dufton Pike, fill the eastern skyline. Turn left, 400yds/m from Little Salkeld, at a black and white road sign, on to a Tarmac and stone track travelling north and then north-east for 800yds/m, suddenly to encounter the Neolithic gigantic stone circle of Long Meg and her Daughters.

One of the largest and most impressive Neolithic stone circles in England, it contains 65 visible stones and is 100 paces in diameter. The circle stones, of hard sandstone, vary in size and shape, with the larger sited at the compass points of north, south, east and west. Long Meg herself stands aloof and out of the circle, an impressive 15ft/4.5m pointing finger of Penrith sandstone, her skirts patterned with cup and ring marks – concentric circles around a dished cup, attributed to 2,500BC and thought to relate to life and death.

Many legends surround Long Meg and her circle, most connected with witchcraft, one being that witch Meg, her daughters and lovers, were turned to stone for blasphemous dancing on the Sabbath.

Leave the pasture containing the stone circle at its waymarked north-east corner, flanked by conifers and cultivated raspberries. Here a series of distinct waymarked gated paths, through pastures and arable fields, leads north-east and north for ³/₄ mile/1.2km to Addingham Church.

The church is reached by crossing Maughanby Lane to a field walkway, making for the churchyard of St. Michael's.

Addingham Church, a 16th-century building, with its external bell tower and hammerhead cross, replaced the original Addingham Church washed away centuries before, in the vicinity of Daleraven Bridge, by the River Eden's change of course.

Leave the church by its main gate, walking east, past former stables for the parish hearse, to the Glassonby road. Turn left and pass two stone barns, Home Farm and Glassonby Hall, between blackberry-laden hedges, before reaching Glassonby, a village of red sandstone, also with Norse connections, being named after a Viking called Glasson. At the Y-junction in the centre of Glassonby, swing left with the lane to Kirkoswald, to leave the houses as the lichen-coated Glassonby Methodist Church, dated 1869, is passed.

The next 1¼ miles/2km, descending north-west with the narrow road, are perhaps the least appealing in the entire walk, as roadside verges are in places non-existent. In its favour are the views and the hedge-rows of cherry, hazel, wild rose and, particularly in season, raspberries and blackberries. Glassonby Beck and Daleraven Bridge are eventually met, and it is here that the waymarked footpath to Lacy's Caves and Little Salkeld plunges left into an ascending plantation of larch and Scots pine. Rise with the left fork and, by a stile, enter a pasture high above the wide waters of the River Eden, a sure guide for most of the return journey. Descending, the way passes through stiled pastures and waterside woodlands for a most pleasing, though in places slithery, stretch to the half-hidden Caves of Lacy. Here, the riverside path rises and curves left over a red sandstone spur, with views ahead of the river and Long Meg viaduct, before sloping right by an outcrop topped with beech and oak.

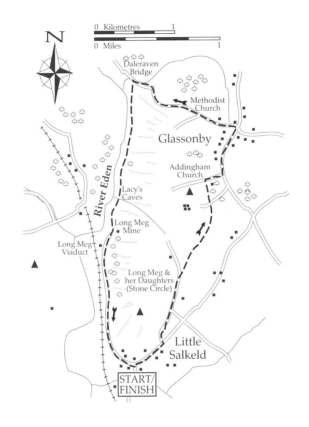

Note a thin permissive path on the right and a notice on the sandstone "Lacy's Caves: This is a dangerous path with sheer drops, please take care with young children. Proceed at your own risk". This notice does not exaggerate; the path is narrow, the vertical drop is substantial, and the river below fast flowing.

Lacy's Caves, hewn out of the soft sandstone in the 1700s, are named after Colonel Lacy, the owner of Salkeld Hall and estates. Five rooms with connecting, pointed arches overlook the river. As to the purpose of the caves, they may have been constructed as a wine cellar or simply as a romantic ruin: gardens surrounded them, for garden shrubs still remain.

From the caves, continue south-west through Cave Wood, with its venerable oak and beech, on the miners' track that ran from Kirkoswald to Long Meg Mine. Pass Force Mill, an old water-powered grain mill on the opposite bank, and the remains of an old tramway that supplied 19th-century mines. As the way closes up on the spectacular viaduct, the river loops away to the right and the route is funnelled through the old rail sidings and approach roads of Long Meg Mine.

Long Meg Viaduct, built in the 1870s for the Settle to Carlisle line, is 60ft/18m high, with seven pillars, and took four years to construct.

Long Meg Mine, the latest and the last of the local gypsum mines, operated alongside the Eden from the 1800s to 1973. Gypsum for the production of plaster of Paris, and anhydrite for sulphuric acid were mined from this minehead. The partially-demolished mine buildings can be seen from the path.

South of the mine a lane, closed to unauthorised vehicles, runs close to the scenic Settle to Carlisle railway line, and guides the walker back to journey's end at Town End Farm, Little Salkeld.

5 Gelt Mill and Talkin Tarn

The varied abundance of wildlife along this circular walk will delight nature lovers, particularly in the woodlands of Geltdale. This gentle journey can be completed wearing well-soled trainers; a Landranger map to identify the rising Pennines will add to the enjoyment.

Distance:
7³⁄₄ miles/12.4km

Height gain:
243ft/74m

Walking time:
3¹⁄₂ hours

Start/Finish:
Talkin. GR549574: 1¹⁄₄ miles/2.8km north of Castle Carrock and, via the B6413, 3¹⁄₄ miles/5.2km south-south-east from Brampton.

Type of walk:
A pastoral journey that allows tantalising glimpses of the North Pennine fells. The waymarked way travels by grassy public paths, country lanes and prepared waterside paths.

Limited parking by the village church, but not at service times.

Talkin, a charming village on the North Pennine fringe, sets the scene for this taster of things to come.

From the church pass by a converted Wesleyan Chapel (1870), and leave Talkin by the side of the Blacksmith's Arms via waymarked stone steps and public footpath (signposted "High Gelt Bridge"). From here the way passes, by copse and marked gated fields, south via Hill House, to the stiled B6413, above High Gelt Bridge. Cross the stone bridge, above a sandstone channel gouged deep by the mad spates of the River Gelt, and turn right at the public bridleway (signposted to Greenwell).

The turbulent River Gelt, much given to seasonal spates, thunders in from the King's Forest of Geltdale. Its name, thought to originate from "geilt" an Irish word meaning mad, was brought to the North Pennines by Norsemen domiciled in Ireland.

A stony and grass road leads north-west to the restored buildings of Greenwell hamlet and Gelt Mill. Alongside one small cottage, a stone stile (Low Gelt) directs right, on to the tree-lined banks of the Gelt, a constant companion for the next 2 miles/3.2km. The way winds over a succession of field stiles on to a short stretch of Tarmac joining the road bridge as it squirms beneath the arches of Middle Gelt viaduct.

Warm, red sandstone houses cluster beneath the viaduct; note the datestone "GTS 1771". One was a coaching inn, the Graham's Arms, that finally called time in the 1970s. The adjoining road bridge, built in 1723 and widened in 1867, enabled the dead of Talkin to be buried in Hayton, rather than distant Brampton.

The railway viaduct, its three arches examples of "skew-arched" bridge building, was completed in 1835, a fact recorded in Latin on the south pillar and in English on the northern pillar – "Francis Giles Sibble, Engineer; John Clyde, Builder".

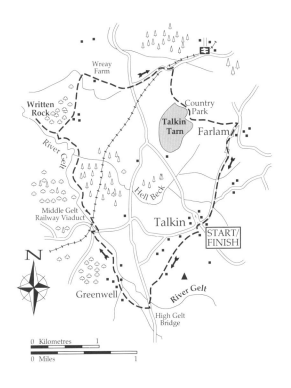

Cross the road bridge north, turning left at the wicket gate ("Public Footpath Gelt Woods"), on to an undulating prepared path that winds north-west with the Gelt, through a colourful mix of broadleaves and scrub. A path, alive with the sights and sounds of waterside and woodland birds, leads to a small stone bridge over Hell Beck.

Encouraged by the tree and waterside management of the RSPB, wagtails, dippers and goosanders flourish, as do thrushes, finches, warblers and woodpeckers. In 1570, Hell Beck ran red with combatants' blood, when 3,000 men and women, fighting for Mary Queen of Scots, lost a bloody battle against the cavalry of England's Queen Elizabeth.

Beyond the bridge, a stepped ascent leads to the drilled and chiselled sandstone cliffs of Brampton Freestone Quarry.

High cliffs of St. Bees sandstone, formed in Triassic times, some 200 million years ago, rise silently skywards, interspersed with bands of coloured shales. The Romans quarried in these parts, and much of Brampton was built with stone from this quarry.

Continue north-west with the main rock- and root-lined pathway, ascending and descending above the twisting gorge of the Gelt to a major fork in the track – Low Gelt, left; Brampton, right. The route to Talkin Tarn is via the right fork, but an interesting short diversion allows sight of Abraham's Cave and the Roman Written Rock of Gelt by taking the left fork, then returning to the path for Brampton.

Abraham's Cave, in the south bank of the Gelt, has a very unromantic history, being hewn in 1814 by Abraham Bird, a gamekeeper, for the purpose of spying on poachers. The Written Rock of Gelt, however, has a much grander pedigree. North of the river, above a causeway, the Written Rock bears details, difficult to decipher, of quarrying by the 2nd Legion for nearby Hadrian's Wall.

The pathway that rises on the Brampton fork, just beyond the ornamental seat beneath the beeches, carries indicators that lead right, via stile and pasture to Unity Farm. Beyond, a walled lane spears right (north and east) to Wreay Farm and its waymarked gated lonnen east to the B6413, a walkway that offers inviting views to the right of the rising Pennine fells. Cross the B6413 to the stone rail bridge, beyond which a kissing gate leads right, on to a footpath, by fence and beech tree, to the boathouse at Talkin Tarn.

The dark waters of Talkin Tarn are cold beyond belief, for it is fed, via a maze of tunnels, from the nether regions of Cold Fell. When the earth was young and the people of Talkin were sinful, God sent an emissary to mend their evil ways; sadly he was rejected by the village. That is, all bar one old lady, who alone was saved when the village and sinners were engulfed by the waters of a cold black tarn. Legend has it that the tarn can talk, but only to those who care to listen to the drowned church bells. Is this cautionary tale the source of its name? Or is it derived from the Celtic "tal" meaning brow and "can" meaning brilliant?

At the waterside, swing left on the arrowed path, as it winds with the tree-lined banks east and south, as far as Post 8. Here, trees and tarn are left as the way passes through a kissing gate, marked "Farlam", on to a narrow trod by fence, pasture and gorse to the gated junction of Farlam. Take the immediate right, passing a farm and a restored cottage to follow the narrow lane for the final stretch south to Talkin.

WEST AND EAST ALLEN DALE

The River West Allen, the River East Allen, and the River Allen all flow into the River South Tyne east of Bardon Mill, yet there are only two dales, West Allen Dale and East Allen Dale. The two dales and the gorge of the River Allen provide a Y-shaped contrast of countryside with few equals in these northern hills, ranging from the dark and grim southern rim of West and East Allen Dales, through the green and flowering meadows of lower valley floors, to the tree-lined tightness of the River Allen Gorge from Cupola Bridge to Allen Banks.

Running south to north for approximately 12 miles/ 19.2km, from the black bastion that is Killhope Law, both dales, so similar yet so subtly different, meet below Whitfield for a joint surge through a winding gorge, before joining the River South Tyne. They have much to offer those who desire the wild open fells or the tree-lined narrows of the River Allen, with the added advantages of the comforts of Allendale Town, or the friendly hostel at Ninebanks.

Isolated and now deserted, with only Allendale Town and Allenheads as population centres – and they have dwindled to a quarter in the last 150 years – the twin dales now appear as a wilderness frontier. Indeed, Allendale Town, the centre of Allen Dale's one-time prosperous lead and silver industry, has never lost its frontier feel. The Enclosure Act of 1792 assisted Allen Dale's agriculture, which prospered alongside the lead and silver boom. In 1851, a silver ingot of 345kgs was sent from Allendale to the Crystal Palace Exhibition, and in 1869, 1^1/$_2$ metric tonnes of silver were recovered from the lead ore of East and West Allen Dale. Sadly, the industry began its slow *but inevitable decline in the mid-1800s, leaving farming as the main employer.*

Lead mining, although it left many scars, such as the ever-present spoil heaps, the Allendale flues, and crumbling chimneys, has, for the walker, provided many fine miles of miners' tracks and carriers' ways over these endless and inviting fells.

Roads have never been in abundance in the Allen Dales, prompting John 'Tar' McAdam to record in 1823 "The roads are altogether the worst that have come to my knowledge". Today, the A686 slices through the lower dale on its way from Hexham to Alston, the B6295 and the B6305 link Allendale Town with the A686, and the B6295 connects Allendale Town with Allenheads, and Cowshill in Weardale. In West Allen Dale, two unclassified roads join to journey south over Coalcleugh Moor and Black Hill to Nenthead.

6 The Gorge of Allen

*There is no gorge in the North Pennines as fine as
Allen Gorge, where tree-clad banks and rocky overhangs channel a twisting 5 miles/8km flow of the
River Allen north. Although a narrow circuit, the
walk can be converted into a linear journey to
Cupola Bridge. The circuit may be, for the dedicated fell-man, somewhat claustrophobic, but for
others it is a woodland wonderland, providing
many forest and waterway flora and fauna, plus
items of historical interest.*

Distance:
9 miles/14.4km

Height gain:
951ft/290m

Walking time:
5 hours

Start/Finish:
Allen Banks Car Park
and Picnic Area.
GR797640: adjoining
Ridley Hall, ½ mile/
1.2km south, by minor
road, from the South
Tyne and the A69(T)
east of Bardon Mill.

Type of walk:
The Allen Gorge offers
several waymarked
paths, forest tracks and
two suspension
footbridges, and on three
occasions rises steeply to
viewpoints and places of
interest on the upper
rim.

The Allen Banks Car Park and Picnic Area, converted from a former walled garden, provides a facilitated start/finish (information, maps – note the position of "Bone Floor"– and lavatories).

From the car park set off south, past an information board and picnic area on to a riverside path.

Trees of many species provide company on this four-seasons journey, a trek that is at its best in the verdant explosion of spring, or in the dying flames of autumn. Allen Banks, gifted to the National Trust by the Bowes-Lyon family, contains 194 acres of long-established hill, crag and riverside scenery, supporting many birds, animals and flowers.

After 800yds/m alongside the west bank of the River Allen, a sagging, but secure, suspension footbridge is met and crossed. Take the middle of three wild garlic-lined paths, ascending steeply east through oak and beech on a stepped zigzag that is waymarked ("Tarn") by stones and by wooden posts. With encroaching paths and tracks, the way becomes somewhat of a maze; this is overcome by continuous ascent by paths only, in an overall easterly direction.

Morralee Tarn is a delightful but small man-made tarn, overgrown by rush, white water lily, and other aquatic plants. Surrounding the tarn are larch and Scots pine, with silver birch at its eastern end.

Descend north from the east end of the tarn on a steep and curving path, where the surrounding lichens, mosses, fungi and ferns indicate a plentiful supply of water – heed well the placement of the feet. Dropping west all the while, the path eventually joins the way of ascent prior to the bridge. Once across turn left (south), for a further wooded trek, of 1 mile/1.6km, by the boulder-strewn waters of the Allen, to Plankey Mill. Pass en route the mighty weather-worn sandstone overhangs of Raven's Crag, and the majestic conifers on the boundary of the Briarwood Bank and Kingswood Nature Reserve, administered by the Northumberland Wildlife Trust. An informative panel by the first footbridge displays woodland and wildlife information.

Glimpses of Plankey Mill Farm and a suspension bridge quicken the step on to a standard footbridge over Kingswood Burn, prior to the ten stone steps leading on to the swaying suspension bridge over the River Allen.

Immediately the east bank is reached, turn right on to a stiled and waymarked permissive path, leading south along the fringes of two pastures, into a stand of regimented conifers. Swing right with the forest track, which narrows into a path, and at every waymarked fork take the right-hand path. Such a route provides a passage, either at the riverside or invariably within sight of the Allen, through the ever-narrowing wooded gorge. For 2 miles/3.2km, this undulating path provides changing views, before finally rising high above an elbow in the river, to reach a fenced pasture on the forest edge, where a waymarked stile leads north.

For those wishing to visit Cupola Bridge, swing right and go back into the trees for a sharp short descent to the attractive bridge over the busy A686. A return up the steep path to the waymarked stile must be made if the circuit is to be completed.

Once over the stile turn left, and follow the faintest of trods alongside the trees to reach and cross a wooden

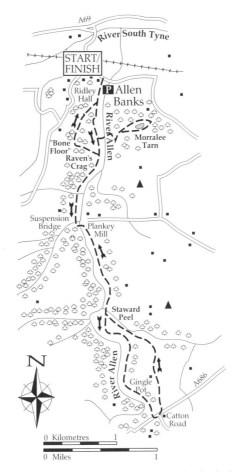

step stile on to the A686. Here, a quick roadside dash, left by the Catton road embankment to a solitary house, is recommended. Opposite the house a decrepit field gate warns of the resident bull, and at the same time allows public passage on to a grassy track north to the ruin of Gingle Pot. Once past the old farm the well-guided raised way continues north to meet a band of trees on the right. Ignore the waymark leading right into the trees, swinging left instead with a curving field track, to enter the forest ahead by stile, National Trust sign and a clump of silver birch.

This is a high heathery ridgeway, with steep and severe drops to the River Allen and Harsondale Burn. Stay on the path until well past the ruins of Staward Peel. By an outcrop of boulders the cover opens for a spectacular view west of the Crooks of Allen, some 260ft/80m below.

Staward Peel is a medieval defensive structure of stone, some purloined from nearby Roman stations, with a gate, portcullis and drawbridge. By the size of its north wall, it was a somewhat grander peel (or pele) than those lining the Scottish Borders. Early occupants were William de Swinburne in 1278, and later, the freebooter "Dicky of Kingswood".

Continue north, descending steeply on what can be a slithery path, to join the outward track on the gorge floor leading to Plankey Mill. Cross the bridges, walking north to re-enter National Trust land, and once the path crosses the incoming Hoods Burn, take the next stepped path left. This steep but short ascent goes through red squirrel country to the quaintly named "Bone Floor" viewpoint.

A short walk north with the descending ridge returns to the outward riverside path and Allen Banks Car Park.

7 West Allen Dale

Although the perimeter fells surrounding Ninebanks do not rise more than 938ft/286m above the River West Allen, the height gain on this walk exceeds this, due to the crossing of two deep-gouged watercourses. The route provides a wide diversity of scenic and wildlife interests, as it journeys through this haunting, little-known dale. As some of the fell paths are indistinct, map and compass skills are needed. Should time be at a premium, the walk can be divided into two, offering a fell trek or a valley floor ramble.

Distance:
10 1/4 miles/16.4km

Height gain:
1,332ft/406m

Walking time:
5 hours

Start/Finish:
Ninebanks Youth Hostel. GR772514: West Allen Dale, 1 3/4 miles/2.8km south-west of Ninebanks, and 1 1/4 miles/2km south from the A686.

Type of walk:
A figure-of-eight moorland and valley walk traversing waymarked pasture and burnside paths, country lanes, carriers' ways and public paths over open fell.

This one-time lead miner's cottage, with views of the walk, provides a fine introduction to exploration of West Allen Dale.

From the hostel walk north, past Raby Cottage, for 440yds/m to the junction of Keirsleywell Row.

Ninebanks Hostel, named Orchard House, occupies what was a miner's cottage and the mine shop of Keirsleywell Level. Small and atmospheric, this haven is a place where all can rest and have their "crack".

As the lane swings right, an old trade and mine track rolls in from Alston, via the Northumbrian county boundary and White Hill. Take this stony, walled and gated byway as it ascends south-west for 2¼ bracing miles/3.6km over the heather flanks of White Hill to the boundary line at Long Cross. After the first mile the guiding walls peter out and the now grassy track swings right, by a stout post, to contour between the seemingly endless fells of Ouston and Mohope. Cross the cleavage of Sandyford Sike by a bridge of 38 wooden sleepers, prior to the gated wall/fence at Long Cross leading into the conifers of Cumbria. With no Long Cross in sight, could this name have referred to yet another boundary cross of the County Palatine of Durham?

At Long Cross turn sharp left and ascend south on a thin and peaty path by fence and wall, through several wet patches of vigorous rushes, to the domed summit of Hard Rigg. The top, however, remains pleasingly dry, as an incoming fence and trig pillar are approached.

Hard Rigg (1,791ft/546m) offers views near and far, from the distant Cheviots to the nearby massif of Cross Fell. The

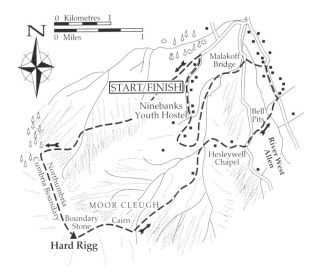

boundary stone at the summit fence and wall junction has a "W" on its north side, "H" on the south side and "91" or "16" on its top. A map of the 1560s indicates that "W" marks the Whitfield estates, "H" the Hawkup estates; the number refers to the year of the enclosures.

From the trig pillar continue south-east to a pole-marked stone stile in the wall, and from there gaze east over the empty moorland by Carrier's Hill. Two lines of naked peat mark the source of Mohope Burn ahead, with a faint and thin trod (marked on maps as a public path) crossing the moss brocks (peat hags), bisecting the faint Carrier's Way, before contouring east below a conspicuous cairn above Moor Cleugh. Once across the deep cleugh, the track traverses north-east over the long ridge of Halley Moor, descending to the abandoned steading of Appletree

Shield, and the three-walled ruin of Hesleywell Chapel at the confluence of Mohope and Wellhope Burns.

[To effect the shorter version of this walk, ascend left to Nether House, then north to Redheugh, swinging left and right with the lane to return to the hostel.]

Turn right, via the footbridge over Wellhope Burn, ascending left with the waymarked track through a wicket gate, leading with a fence/wall to the extensive modern steading of Hesleywell Farm. Pass between the two largest buildings and cross the yard on to the signposted road to Nether Harsley. From here a pasture path ascends south-east to yet another derelict farm before swinging east, via stile and gate, on to a track leading to the inhabited house, Middle Gate. The public path passes into the drive, between house and outhouse, to cross a small wall stile leading to a waymarked descent east to Broadlee.

Turn left, walking north for about 220 paces, to leave the lane, right, entering a strip of pine and broadleaves. Near the end of this shelter belt, enter a pasture and descend north-east to a gate ahead leading steeply to the River West Allen. Its stony and carboniferous banks are crossed by a footbridge – note the adjacent bell pits – before taking the right-hand of two gates, and, with a stile, ascending right, through the trees. On emerging from the trees, a steep pasture rises to the roadway by Greenleycleugh Farm (1689).

Turn left on to roadside verges, to reach Farneyside Cottages. At the northern end of the cottages by a wall stile, prior to the house of Bates Hill, a signpost directs the walker west alongside a descending gully, to cross the West Allen by a footbridge. Beyond, an ascent left to gateposts, then a diagonal crossing, reaches a lane dropping to Malakoff Bridge, over the rock-strewn bed of Mohope Burn.

The bridge is named after, and built at the time of, the Crimean battle of Malakoff, the second such occurrence of the name in the North Pennines.

Immediately beyond the bridge, pass through a gate on the left, on to the middle track of three, crossing the pasture south to gain gated access to Mohope Burn, along its northern bank. Continue with the burn, and its wildlife, as far as the confluence on the right with Blind Burn, which is forded, and then followed by ascending the small ridge south. Note the many spoil heaps over Blind Burn to beyond Keirsleywell Row and the youth hostel. The waymarked and gated way between the two burns, home to one of the local bulls, soon reaches, by stone stile, the flower-bedecked cottage of Redheugh, leading, via its front drive, to an angled lane. Turn right on to the lane walking west, then right again, rising north for the final steps to Ninebanks Hostel.

*Evidence of prolonged mining activity surrounds the area of the hostel. Bell pits, hushes, horse levels, spoil heaps, mine shops and miners' cottages can all be seen. And records show that lead ore was mined as early as the mid-1500s at Keirsleywell (*A History of Lead Mining in the Pennines, *Raistrick and Jennings). Three mines, Keirsleywell Horse Level, Mohope Head and Scraithole Mine, were developed around the area of today's hostel and this walk.*

8 Coalcleugh and Carrshield

Walking on the roof of the North Pennines, where space, solitude, distant vistas, and colourful wildlife abound, is a breathtaking experience. This fine circuit is an outstanding example, but do stick to the recommended route, because much of West Allen Dale is riddled with half-hidden mine shafts and sink holes.

Distance:
8¼ miles/13.2km

Height gain:
1,063ft/324m

Walking time:
5 hours

Start/Finish:
Coalcleugh. GR802452: at the junction of the unclassified Allenhead Town to Nenthead and the Allenheads to Nenthead roads, 2 miles/3.2km north-east from Nenthead, and 1¾ miles/2.8km south of Carrshield.

Type of walk:
This airy and scenic circular walk encompasses the highs and lows of West Allen Dale head. Miners' and carriers' tracks ease ascent, although in places nature has obscured these old ways.

Car parking on the roadside lay-by at the junction.

Coalcleugh, at the dark dale-head, its flanks and banks crimped by the hand of the galena-gatherers, is the alpha and omega of this adventure.

Coalcleugh Level, worked from 1729, was one of the first lead mines to use locomotives underground. Manufactured in Germany by the Schram Engineering Company, they replaced the "trammers" and their ponies in 1912.

Walk west, from the lay-by and roadside house, on a waymarked and, initially, gated mine track, passing an abandoned house/mine shop of Coalcleugh Level amidst a scatter of spoil heaps. The wide track fords the sandstone of Alston Cleugh, above its tiny linn, to meet a waymarked fork ahead; here it swings left (west), rising through grassed-over spoil. Underfoot it narrows to a thin grass path ascending with a series of strategically-placed (on the skyline ahead) posted waymarks. To the right the rounded dome of The Dodd rises quietly above Dodd's End before the gated boundary wall of Northumberland and Cumbria is met.

Do not pass through the gate but turn right (north) with the wall about 150 paces to a waymarked post. Then, gradually leaving the wall, cross the tussocky fell a degree or two east of north to a marked post ahead in the hillside. This is the first of several indicators that wind north with an old grassed mine track, providing the easiest of ascents over the eastern heights of The Dodd.

As height is gained on The Dodd, the pastoral and lonely dale of West Allen opens up to the north. The upper reaches are a delight in the soft warmth of summer, a wilderness in winter's grip. Note the Bhuddist monastery by Wolfcleugh and Limestone Brae.

With what appears to be half of Northumberland laid out ahead, the grooved way surges north along this fine ridgeway, gradually descending over Smallburns Moor, past a crosspath finger post, where each of the four is labelled "Public Bridleway". The north path leads to The Nook, the east to Carrshield and the west over Wellhope Moor to Nenthead. Ahead, slightly left, a prominent cairn marks a change of direction and the loss of the definite path. When the cairn is passed, walk north-north-west over the fell for 800yds/m to the angled wall enclosing the upper grazing above Wellhope Mine, Rough Tongue and Wellhope, a side dale of West Allen.

For the next 1½ miles/2.4km, this northbound wall and accompanying path/track make navigation easy, as the way bounds over Middle Rigg and Quarry Hill to descend a gated track to the Tarmac by Middle Gate. At the signposted lane turn sharp right, pass through the gate and descend south-east past the converted buildings of The Nook.

Continue with the lane, ascending with the right fork to the tree-sheltered steading of Farney Shield on the immediate skyline. Beyond, a gated lane leads south-west on to the extensive acres of rough grazing, quaintly shown on the map as "The Bottoms". The public path, although distinct at first, soon deteriorates as descent continues south-east; a good marker is the tree-lined riverside hamlet of Carrshield. As the barely visible Black Cleugh, trickling in from The Meres above, is reached, swing left and make for a gate in the left-hand wall.

Pass through, into a pasture and descend east, with Black Cleugh, to another gate leading on to stepped stones, dropping to a footbridge over the River West

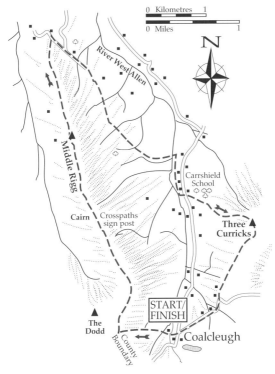

Allen below Whiteley Shield Farm. An attractive waterside way now leads right (south) for nearly 800yds/m to another footbridge at Carrshield. Do not cross, but turn left with a stepped path, and ascend between henhouses and a scatter of white-washed cottages by the roadside drying green and parking area in Carrshield.

Carrshield school was built in 1851 "At the instigation of and on land belonging to B Beaumont Esq., for the education of children of all religious denominations." A bell tower and separate classrooms for boys and girls still remain. Beaumont was the proprietor of the Blackett-Beaumont Company in Allendale and Weardale.

Depart from the village, via the signpost ("Carrshield Moor 1 mile") immediately opposite the point of emergence, by a cobbled way, to enter and ascend the two right-hand pastures leading south-east to deserted Loudside. A jumble of small pens and buildings are negotiated via a maze of single gates, to a stoned track on the open fell. Turn right for a very brief acquaintance with the track, leaving it left, south-south-east, on a grassy groove rising through the quarry spoil above. The contour lines and the path narrow as the way climbs above a north-south line of disused quarries. The line is followed to its southern end above High Blue Row – converted miners' cottages/mine shops – where a wide grass track is met rising east from the valley floor.

The public bridleway to Carrshield Moor crosses this wide way and continues its gradual climb south-south-east over open moorland to a solitary waymarked pole on the skyline ahead.

From the curricks, descend south for 250yds/m on to a peat and sandy path, and turn right to meet the waymarked pole. Turn right (south-west), to stride down a distinct pathway, passing the fallen stones of Rushyman and Whetstoneman, to the Allenheads road by Bridge Cleugh. And with the roadside verge, walk west beyond Mutton Hall to journey's end and one last lingering look to the lonely fells and walled pastures of West Allen Dale.

9 Allendale Chimney Stacks

This journey quickly sets the North Pennine scene, for these upland stretches of the Allens' twin dales not only provide characteristic sights and sounds of the North Pennines, but also include unique examples of smelt mill flues and chimney stacks. The walk offers invigorating miles, with a few ascents and interest for all.

Distance:
11 miles/17.6km

Height gain:
1,404ft/428m

Walking time:
5-5½ hours

Start/Finish:
Allendale Town. GR837558: 11 miles/ 17.6km south-west of Hexham via the B6305, B6304 and B6303, and 7½ miles/12km north of Allenheads via the B6295.

Type of walk:
A testing fell-top figure-of-eight hike to and from East Allen Dale and West Allen Dale. Underfoot a mix of country lanes, good fell tracks, narrow fell trods and waymarked pasture paths.

Parking for vehicles in the Market Place.

Allendale – suffixed Town – with its village hall, is an ideal terminal from which to start, a place of interest that warrants inspection.

From the Market Place walk west on the Peth-Thornley Gate/Ninebanks road, spiralling down to cross Mill Bridge over the River Allen.

Allendale Town, gateway to the North Pennines, was granted its original charter by Edward I, when it was known as "Allenton". This market town and centre for the lead mining industry of East and West Allen Dales, has had a colourful history and still retains that "frontier town" feeling.

Legacies from the Romans, the reivers and, more recently, the lead and silver mines abound. In the 1800s, the boom time, Allendale had a population of 6,500 and a reputation for flamboyant living, hence the predominance of inns and ale houses. The miners were paid six-monthly, and these biennial occasions, known as "The Pays", attracted traders and villains alike to what was inevitably a week of whoopee. The old-time fun still lives on in "Tar Barling" on Old Year's Night, when flaming tar barrels, carried on the heads of guisers, are hurled on to the Market Place bonfire as the New Year bells sound.

Once across and past Bridge End Mill, turn sharp left, passing through a cluster of attractive cottages, including the Friends' Meeting House, to take the first right, ascending on to a narrow lane.

The first Meeting House of the Society of Friends (Quakers) was built in 1733 and rebuilt in 1870; note the burial ground and the "privies" built over the burn.

Beyond the tidy farmhouse (1760), swing left rising steadily by Wager House. At the next fork keep right

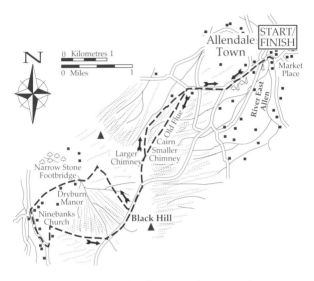

(west), by a tree-filled gully, ascending over the cross-roads to a Y-junction by Frolar Meadow Farm. Bear left, up the walled and gated lane, to reach the open fell, swinging left on a grassy track curling south to join the old flue line from Allen Mill. A pathway, alongside the now derelict flue, rises straight and steady to the smaller chimney, passing a cemented stone cairn with a missing plaque en route. Continue to the second and originally larger chimney, via a wide pathway and flue line.

The chimney stacks that stand in glorious isolation on the North Pennines' skyline, were an essential part of the "Reverberatory Furnace" system operated in the larger lead smelt mills. This process required a controllable draught, supplied by a high chimney on a high site, at the end of a long flue.

The lower of the two amputated Allendale chimneys, fed by a single flue, has a base circumference of 63ft/19m; the higher, with two flues, has a measurement of 96ft/29m. (NOTE: Chimneys and flues are dangerous and should be observed, not examined.)

From the chimneys, a southbound, prepared path leads to a signposted wicket gate on the Allendale-Nenthead road. Pass through and continue south to a roadside public bridleway post. Turn right for a scenic north-west traverse of Dryburn Moor, aided by arrowed posts as far as the stone wall. Swing right with the wall to a small ruined stone shelter, turning left through the gated stone wall on to a thin pasture path, dropping to the sad ruin of Dryburn Manor (surely a misnomer). A cart track contours right to the tree line, and crosses Dry Burn on what must be the narrowest of stone footbridges in the North Pennines. Rise to skirt a working farm and, with the track west, meet yet another deserted steading. At this point leave the track, left, for a gated public path through three walled pastures to Ninebanks Church.

On the road, below the church and above West Allen River, turn left, rising with the Tarmac for 800yds/m to the house of Spartywell and an old limekiln.

At the kiln, take a sharp turn left (north) on to a crumbling public byway, which, although steep, is ascended with some ease to a tree-lined fork. Swing right (east), on a walled track by some Scots pine to a wooden gate opening on to Dryburn Moor. Here an arrowhead indicates a thin rush-bound trod east to the grassed-over shafts and spoil on the immediate skyline. Ahead (east), 800yds/m of unmarked rough grass and heather fell, requiring a sense of direction and compass skills, leads to the Nenthead-Allendale road.

The roadside snow poles make good markers, and once reached, turn left on to the roadside verge for an elevated 1 mile/1.6km hike to the gate and prepared path by the now visible chimney, a hike that allows a bird's-eye view down the Dry Burn into West Allen Dale. From the larger and higher (elevation) of the two crumbling chimneys descend, initially north then north-east, alongside the left-hand and more complete flue, on the panoramic Carrier's Way to Fell House.

The arched Allendale flues, one 2¼ miles/4.1km long, the other a mere 110yds/m shorter, carried out to the letter the original suggestion, published in 1778 by Bishop Watson, to purify the air around the smelt mills. A long flue from furnace to chimney on a nearby hill would not only cause the lead fumes to condense and save a considerable amount of recoverable lead, but also make the smoke largely harmless, so reducing the risk of "bellond" (poisonous) ground).

Carrier's Way is a section of a packhorse route from Weardale Head, and no doubt West Allendale, to the Allen Smelt Mill.

Continue past the shepherd's cottage of Fell House on a wide track, which, beyond the gate, becomes a Tarmac lane leading to a Y-junction – the outward route from Allendale Town. Take the right fork (east), past the farm for the final descent, continuing east at the next crossroads, as the tree-lined lane wends its downward way. Pass the warm stones of Wager House, before swinging right on to a narrow lane prior to crossing Mill Bridge. The Peth may rise steeply, but succour is at hand.

10 Holms Linn

This pastoral ramble reveals the gentle side of East Allen Dale, so aptly expressed by J. Ritson,

Allendonia! fair and wild!

If sometimes stern yet often mild.

The occasional ascents are always short, and breath can be regained while admiring the surrounding views and the resident wildlife.

Distance:
3½ miles/5.6km

Height gain:
394ft/120m

Walking time:
2 hours

Start/Finish:
Sinderhope Community Centre. GR845521: on the B6295, 3 miles/4.8km south of Allendale Town and 5 miles/8km north from Allenheads. A car park stands alongside the centre.

Type of walk:
A short low-level circular walk that pleases the eye, on waymarked waterside and pasture paths, country lanes, farm tracks and a goodly number of various stiles.

Walk north across the old school-yard, leaving via a wicket-gate beneath a solitary sycamore, to descend with the right-hand fence and guiding stile to the Acton road.

The school was built in 1856 by W.B. Beaumont MP, aided by local public subscriptions, for the education of children of all religious denominations. It was extended in 1881.

Acton road is crossed by stile and wicket-gate. With a wide grassy path, descend to the north bank of the River East Allen, where, aided by more gates and stiles, the riverside pathway soon reaches the tumbling cascade of Holms Linn. Here a recent footbridge (1984) assists the river crossing and provides a viewing platform for the surging linn.

Although the fall over the Whin Sill step is barely 15ft/5m, the flow is wide and well-proportioned, and the whole is enhanced by a surrounding frame of overhanging trees. Holms Linn is a hidden gem.

Once over the bridge, step on to the south bank to follow it west, with the waymarks, passing the remaining surface accessories of the Blackett Level and Holms Linn Shaft.

The Blackett Level, a long adit (a crosscut tunnel/level) was constructed to aid drainage and exploration of the lead-rich Allenheads workings. Instigated in 1855 by T. Sopwith, agent for the Blackett-Beaumont Company, work started in 1859 from Allendale Town, when three shafts were sunk along its course, one of which was the Holms Linn Shaft, 2 1/4 miles/3.6km from the Allendale Town portal, and 340ft/104m deep. Work stopped in 1896, with few discovered veins, 4 1/4 miles/7.2km of level, and an astronomical outlay of £120,000.

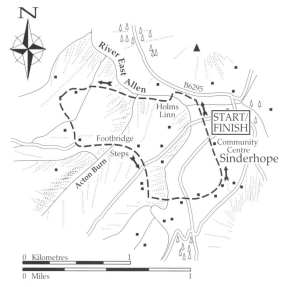

Continue west with the picturesque riverbank, crossing the incoming Acton Burn by a footbridge, to rise and leave the river on a steep and slithery bracken-clad path. Once on to the hillock, a four-way signpost is met. Continue west over a wee footbridge to Crowberry Hall Farm. Pass with care through the yard, and then turn left on to the well-waymarked field-side way, south and east, to Low Acton Farm.

Although some valley floor farm fields are given over to arable farming, many produce winter fodder in the traditional way. By delaying the cutting of the hay meadow until after flowering, farmers ensure the continued inclusion and regeneration of the many flowering and nutritious plants. Visit the Pennine dales in colourful June.

From Low Acton descend east into Acton Burn dene, via waymarked stiles to cross a small footbridge and ascend right, south-east, and then south, by wobbly steps and pasture fields to a roadside Wesleyan Methodist Chapel (1861), now used as a barn by Pry Hill Farm. Further waymarked stiles lead to the east side of Pry Hill's steading. Turn right and follow the fence past the farmhouse, walking south to the gated corner of the field.

Here the waymarks and the paths run out for a short distance. Pass through the gate, swing right, descending steeply south-east and south through scrub and tangly grass, to the two visible and waymarked footbridges below. They cross, first Hob Sike and then the merry waters of East Allen, enabling the way to jink cleverly around the houses, by narrow stile and stepped path, east into a pasture. This path is not as steep as it first seems, for the B6295 is easily reached by exiting at Broad Gate.

Cross the road and ascend east, via a unique stepped miniature gate, on a public path that wriggles round an occupied cottage and the not-so occupied buildings of High Sinderhope, to reach the working farm of Sinderhope Black House. Before this farm is reached, swing left (north) through a gate, and with a guiding fence on the right, descend through two fields to the B6295 at Sinderhope Centre.

As the final descent is made to Sinderhope Centre, note the sweeping wooded flanks of Holms, as Garret's Hill plunges steeply to the River East Allen. The North Pennines are not entirely, as was stated in the 1790s "mountains frowned with a melancholy sterility and nakedness"; the dale's beauty, as expressed by J. Ritson in the walk's introduction, is "yet often mild."

11 Allenheads and Byerhope

An elevated trail of discovery, this walk shows how the old mining and smelt centre of Allenheads and its surrounds have risen phoenix-like from the ashes of man's indifference to nature. Extensive and revealing views on the high outward journey and a changing habitat on the return make this walk a rewarding experience.

Distance:
5¾ miles/9.2km

Height gain:
650ft/198m

Walking time:
3 hours

Start/Finish:
Allenheads.
GR861454: at the head of East Allen Dale, on the B6295 Allendale Town to Cowshill road, 7½ miles/12km south from Allendale Town, and 3¾ miles/6km north of Cowshill.

Type of walk:
A remarkably easy circuit, traversing the rim of Fawside and Byerhope Bank before descending for an enjoyable riverside return to Allenheads. Underfoot, on country lanes, stony miners' tracks and waymarked fell and riverbank paths.

Parking spaces alongside the Heritage Centre and in the car park opposite.

Allenheads, now a village at peace, provides an ideal start, with both refreshment and local information.

From the Heritage Centre, a mine of information, or the nearby Allenheads Inn, with its rich vein of bric-a-brac, ascend south to the old library, then east with the signposted Rookhope road. Once past Eastend Reservoir and a roadside cairn, leave the tree-lined Tarmac, via a waymarked grassy path, to reach a sign ("Byerhope 2 miles") higher up the curving roadway.

Allenheads Heritage Centre charts the progress of lead and silver mining in this North Pennine village – the highest in England – from the early 1800s. Also on show is the only surviving hydraulic engine built by W.G. Armstrong in 1852, one of nine produced for winding or pumping in the local lead mines.

The heavy-duty track to Byerhope proceeds north-west by an unsightly quarry on the right and a tidy cairn on the left; a place in the gods from which to view the restored village of Allenheads and its re-structured grassed-over surrounds. Once past this machine-made crater, a contouring mine road sweeps over Noble Sike and Middle Rigg before settling down to a wall-assisted route north-north-west over Byerhope Mere, above the shrinking waters of Byerhope Reservoir.

A sprinkling of old, abandoned farms stand forlorn on Middle Rigg, home to the miner/farmer who, with his wife and family, worked both mine and "three acres and a cow". Families subsisted on the "3 Ps" – pig, poultry and pota-toes, but when the bells were heard of the galloway pack-horses, each carrying 16 stone/102 kilos of lead ore from mine to smelt mill, farming stopped, and lead ore was mined.

Smelt mills, on the eastern flanks of the dale, were situated at Ellershope and St. Peter's and on the western flanks at Swin Hope, Struthers and Allenheads Mill.

Note also the reservoirs of Dodd, Coatenhill, Eastend, Springhouse and the larger Byerhope Reservoir (which can be reached from the Allenheads road) that surround Allenheads, man-made lakes that ensured a regular flow of water for the mine machinery.

In his diary for 1857, mines agent Thomas Sopwith wrote, "After tea we (W.G. Armstrong, Mr Kendal and Sopwith) had a pleasant walk to Byrehope (sic), a lovely evening and I was pleased to see several groups of people enjoying themselves in the agreeable promenade by the banks of the reservoir".

Below, left, the working farm of Byerhope can be seen, and ahead by Byerhope Raceground the track leaves the angled wall to reach a conical cairn at a track junction. Swing right, north, as indicated by an arrowhead on the reverse side of the cairn, to a post on the skyline by High Haddock Stones.

High Haddock Stones are a shoal of weather-worn sandstone outcrops that lie some yards north from the track junction above Byerhope Bank. The track of Broad Way that climbs east and north, over the watershed of East Allen Dale and Beldon Burn valley, is worth exploration if time allows, providing far-reaching views east into Rookhopedale and the valley of Beldon Burn.

From the three-arrowed post, descend left on a waymarked grass and dirt pathway that zigzags between a scatter of spoil heaps to the valley floor.

A wicket-gate opens on to the B6295 by Fell View. Cross the road and descend past the cottages to the

River East Allen, spanned by ford and footbridge. Turn left (south) on to the lane alongside the true left bank of the river, leaving the lane by the signpost ("Dirt Pot ¾ mile"). Here a narrow but distinct riverside path, overgrown in places in the summer, winds peacefully between water and wall to join the roadway into the village of Dirt Pot.

The village of Dirt Pot – a deer path, with its strung out rows of miners' cottages and two Methodist chapels, one Wesleyan, one Primitive (The Ranters) – was custom built for workers in this lead mining heartland.

As the last cottage is passed, the narrow road continues south-east alongside the river for the final ¾ mile/ 1.2km into Allenheads. A route that, although pastoral, still bears the scars of its lead mining past.

DERWENTDALE

Short and small, upper Derwentdale nevertheless has much to offer the lover of the great outdoors. Positioned at the north-eastern extremity of the North Pennines, close to Tyneside and the heavier-populated parts of County Durham, it contains, in addition to areas of tranquil tree-clad rivers and gusty open fells, four villages of charm and character and the large Derwent Reservoir.

The county boundary of Northumberland and Durham runs with the River Derwent and its tributary Beldon Burn. Although at its lower reaches the Derwent spills into the Tyne, the waters from the southern flanks of Bolt's Law run into the Wear. The now dammed Derwent, in addition to supplying Tyneside with water, provides many facilities, including a nature reserve, a country park, sailing and picnic areas.

Although the historic villages of Edmundbyers and Blanchland are extremely popular, particularly at week-ends and public holidays, the dale, as it probes deep into the high fells overlooking Rookhopedale, Allen Dale and Devil's Water, provides some of the finest fell walks in the Pennines. Grouse moors abound on Blanchland Fell, as do the regiments of conifers in Slaley Forest.

The B6278 from Stanhope and the B6306 from Hexham, lead into the upper dale, and the A68 passes within a mile or so of Derwent Reservoir and Edmundbyers.

12 Edmundbyers and Pedam's Oak

Never demanding, with inclines of a gentle nature, this rewarding excursion, waymarked in places, is always distinct and easy to traverse, thus allowing the many items of interest to be enjoyed and appreciated.

Distance:
9 miles/14.4km

Height gain:
656ft/200m

Walking time:
4-4 1/2 hours

Start/Finish:
Edmundbyers.
GR017501: straddles
the junction of the
B6306 and the B6278,
5 1/2 miles/8.8km east of
Blanchland, 1 1/2 miles/
2.4km south-west of
Derwent Reservoir,
and 8 miles/12.8km
north from Stanhope.

Type of walk:
A rectangular, open fell
and valley-side journey
of two distinct halves,
offering an invigorating
hike in scenic solitude,
over heathery fell and
upland pastures on
contouring miners'
tracks of stone, grass and
peat.

**Consideration when
parking in the village is
appreciated.**

Edmundbyers, eastern gateway to the North Pennine fells, is an ancient village of character and charm. With inn,

post office/village shop and youth hostel, it provides a
natural start/finish.

From either inn, shop or youth hostel, take the
Blanchland road west, via the village green with its
mix of chestnut, oak, rowan, copper beech, and stone
water troughs, rising to a minor junction at the elbow
ahead. As the road swings sharp right, track left (west),
as indicated by the signpost ("Lead Mining Trail, Public
Footpath").

Edmundbyers is reputed to have been named after King
Edmund the martyr, who in the 9th century took up arms
against the invading Vikings. The youth hostel, circa 1936,
is housed in what was an early 17th-century inn, named
the Low House. From there, a former landlord perished
whilst searching for his wife lost on the surrounding moors.
His ghost, with grey hair and beard, has been seen in the
hostel on several occasions, particularly by visiting
Antipodeans. No sightings, however, have been reported
since a service for young persons, conducted by the Bishop
of Durham, was held in the hostel in 1993.

Follow the dirt and stone track, forking right and then
left, to pass a scatter of rusting agricultural machinery, before descending the gated way to cross Black
Burn. The route then rises sharp left, with sandstone
underfoot, to contour the heather- and bracken-blan-
keted fell to reach and pass alongside the southern
wall of a large pasture enclosure on the right. Ignore
any tracks and paths that from time to time join the
route as it progresses, mainly west, above Limerick
Edge, to zigzag below Swandale Head. A pause and
backward glance, along the valley of Burnhope Burn
and over the roofs of Edmundbyers to the skyline of
Derwentdale, may dispel many misconceptions of
Durham County.

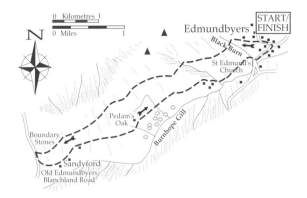

The unmistakable track, over the heathery moors, now surges west-south-west as it gobbles up the miles on this fine ridgeway, eventually to meet at an angled wall a rickety, rudimentary stile alongside a wired gate. Cross the stile with care, swinging half-right on the bisecting path, over the riggs and furrows of a coarse pasture, to reach a small labelled gate that leads once more to the sea of heather on Edmundbyers Common. Bear left (south-west), on a heather-lined sandstone and peat track, rising gently to reach yet another labelled gate.

Beyond, the most practical passage is sharp right with the fenceside track, approaching a line of shooting butts, and at a track junction swing left on to a wide stony track descending to an angled boundary fence and a grassy lay-by alongside the Blanchland/Stanhope road. From here the south-west skyline is dominated by the two chimneys of Sikehead, and beyond, the cone of Bolt's Law with its prominent trig pillar. To the south, the tall communications tower on Horseshoe Hill commands attention.

Boundary stones, situated at intervals, erected under the Commons Enclosure Act of 1800 to mark parish boundaries, can be seen prior to, at and beyond the angle in today's boundary fence. Fashioned from dressed sandstone, in the style of roadside milestones, the one at the fence corner carries the letters "DC" on one side and "LC" on the reverse, with the other two marked "DC" and "GT". Boundary stones seen on Walk 23 also carry the letters "DC". Another item of interest at the boundary corner, although with no explanation, is "The Old Man's Grave", marked by a bedded long stone and a rounded boulder.

From the grass roadside lay-by, walk south-east on what was the original Blanchland to Edmundbyers road. Although overgrown, the close-bedded road stones can be seen, as can the depressions made by many wagon wheels. By the first gate and railed stile the third dressed boundary stone can be seen, as the way continues and links with an incoming miners' track at the padlocked gate ahead. At this point, veer left to begin the low-level pastured return east-north-east above the, at times, steep-sided Burnhope Gill. Compared to the outward half, this section is a total contrast, as it meanders through upland pastures and by six derelict and deserted farmhouses and cottages.

This lower route is also unmistakable, for the cart track widens and its base hardens eventually to merge with the Tarmac. It provides, as it progresses, fine views ahead of the TV tower on Pontop Pike, and of Derwentdale. The route, lined with the farm skeletons of Sandyford and its shieling, then sightless Belmount, house and steading, leads to the sad ruins of the once proud farmhouse of Pedam's Oak, its modern buildings looking somewhat out of place. Finally, once College Sike and College Edge are passed, the stones of College Farm and empty Swandale Cottage, with its brightly painted door and shutters, lead to the valley floor and Limerick Lane.

Pedam's Oak, a farm since 1380, takes its name from a thief who hid in an oak tree close by.

Prior to the small reservoir, on a descending winding road, swing left on to the sand and stone surface of Limerick Lane. A rutted, rising track below Limerick Edge, through bracken, whin and briar banks leads north-east to join the B6278 from Stanhope. Turn left for a short sharp ascent into Edmundbyers, calling at the Saxon church of St. Edmund on the left, before journey's end.

The 12th-century stone building replaced an earlier church of mud, timber and thatch; evidence of Saxon and Norman work was found during the latest restoration. The single stone altar, of a type banned during the Reformation, was missing for over 300 years, but thankfully reappeared and was restored in 1855. Many fine coloured-glass windows can be seen, including one, at the west end, of an eye.

13 Sikehead and Bolt's Law

A diverse journey, not only rich in wildlife, but also exhibiting many visible examples of the area's industrial past, coupled with extensive views from the domed summit of Bolt's Law. For enthusiasts, this walk and Walk 12 can be linked to form an intriguing figure-of-eight.

Distance:
4¼ miles/7.2km

Height gain:
623ft/190m

Walking time:
2-3 hours

Start/Finish:
GR962479: by the Blanchland-Stanhope unclassified road, 1¾ miles/2.8km south from Blanchland, and 7¾ miles/12.4km north-north-west of Stanhope. Limited car parking on the roadside or quarry verges.

Type of walk:
A short circular walk by public paths, grassy and through heather, cart tracks and country lanes. A fell hike for those who require ascents that are short and not too sharp.

A "Lead Mining Trail" signpost by the roadside and above a disused quarry, provides a fine moorland springboard, 1,362ft/415m above sea level, from which to start this bracing circuit. Walk south-south-west to Buckshott Moor, on a grassy path through heather, for 1 mile/1.6km, to a towering grey chimney ahead: a way that meets and walks with the remnants of a disused smelt-mill flue.

Flues, brick/stone arched ducts, ran from the smelt mills at lower levels, often exceeding 2,000 yds/m in length, to chimneys on the high fells. Their purpose was to pipe the noxious emissions from the smelt mills, and at the same time extract vaporised lead from the fumes by allowing it to condense on the brick/stone walls. Pity the poor souls who had to recover the condensed lead, and the moorland wildlife that breathed the sulphurous fumes belching from the chimneys.

As the first chimney is approached, the track swings south through a gate to skirt below the eastern embankment of the man-made Sikehead Dams. These reservoirs provided a regular supply of water, possibly for "hushing" and certainly for power, for the nearby mines. From the southern point of the reservoirs, now home to aquatic birds, continue south-west over a sike to a T-junction of paths; turn right for the second chimney and derelict mine shops of Sikehead, some 200yds/m ahead.

Lead mining, by drift, shaft or hushing, was serviced by an assortment of "mine shops" – buildings or rooms housing the blacksmith, the stables, the mine office, the engines, the jiggers, the stores, and the notorious lodging-shops. Here, three men per bunk, with a boy at the foot, slept in rooms where supper was cooked and clothes were dried.

After a visual, but not hands-on or feet-on, inspection of Sikehead Mine, leave the mine shops and sterile spoil to cross a small sike south, rising to an angled fence and stile close by three very large blocks of dressed, holed stone. With back to the stile, from the winding house blocks the railbed of the grassed-over dismantled railway can be seen contouring south, with Bolt's Law rising darkly to the right.

Ore from Sikehead would be transported to Ramshaw's smelt mills by wagons down the incline to Bolt's Hope, and no doubt "pigs" of lead would return to be loaded on to a branch of the Rookhope line of the old Stanhope and Tyne Railway; the highest standard gauge railway in England.

Stride south with the grassy railbed for 540yds/m to a crossroads, an invigorating stretch that provides expansive views ahead over Stanhope Common. At the crossing of the paths, just prior to a line of shooting butts, leave the railbed by turning right (south-west), to make the final ascent of 800yds/m to the trig pillar crowning the summit of Bolt's Law (1,772ft/540m). As the heather-bound pathway ascends to the summit, note a bisecting track coming in from the right; this is the route of descent, returning from the grandstand of Bolt's Law.

On a clear day the Northumbrian hills can be seen stretching endlessly to the Scottish Border and distant Cheviot, whilst south and west wild Weardale and Rookhopedale lead the eye over Allendale Common.

The summit descent is north-east to the crosspaths, by the 500m contour, then left, descending steadily to the gated desolation below that was Boltshope Fluorspar Mine. At the now derelict mine check-in, by Bolt's Burn, turn right on to a Tarmac road running north,

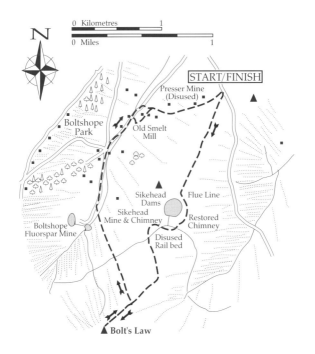

through a thinning avenue of trees, to meet a signposted, forked road at Ramshaw. Take the right fork, to Stanhope, passing the restored properties of Boltslaw Cottage and The Mill, before crossing the bridge over Bolt's Burn and rising with the lane to a cart track forking right.

Ramshaw Smelt Mills, purpose-built furnaces with stone hearths replaced the old baal or bole hills; they in turn were superseded in the early 1700s by coal-fired furnaces that kept the heat source from the ore, using a controlled draft created by a tall mill chimney. Such a system of continuous smelting was developed further by precise temperature control, enabling the processing of more lead and silver.

Two possible routes lead to the public path east of Manor House: (1) continue with the cart track, crossing a narrow road to a field gate opening on to a walled "white" road, rising south to join the public path by Manor House. This white road is marked on maps, but not as a public path; (2) at the road to the cottages turn sharp right to pass the cottages, walking south-west alongside a fenced plantation to a junction of several paths by a clearing, with tin hut and adjacent mine shaft. Turn immediately left to enter the conifers, via a primitive stile, on to a narrow public path in places overgrown by sitka.

Beware the deep shafts, fortunately fenced, that line this route east to forsaken Manor House. Once beyond Manor House, continue east to the next fork, taking the right leg through the gate to rise, on a curving conifer-lined path, to a gated and walled fell. Ahead, a third chimney stack and restored buildings can be seen to the east, and are soon reached via a rush-ridden fell path. The fenced property is now a pumping station for Northumbrian Water; in the past it was the site of Presser Lead Mine.

The 19th-century Presser Lead Mine operated a Cornish steam-driven lifting engine that serviced its two mine shafts. One sank to a depth of 1,000ft/305m and now houses a water pump at 650ft/198m. The stone lining for this shaft contains a fossil tree – Sigillaria species – cast in hard ganister.

The final steps are taken north-east, via a stony road from the pumping station to journey's end, at the Blanchland-Stanhope highway.

14 Baybridge and Riddlehamhope

Solitude and wild beauty are the walker's companions as endless easy trails probe the upper reaches of Derwentdale, and the Carrier's Way contours north over the heathery acres of Bulbeck Common. Along the way, hear the curlew's cry and experience the seldom-seen Devil's Water Valley. Couple that with Blanchland, a gem of a village in the North Pennines' crown, and you have a walk that is simply the best.

Distance:
11 miles/17.6km

Height gain:
804ft/245m

Walking time:
5-5½ hours

Start/Finish:
Baybridge. GR958499: by Beldon Burn in upper Derwentdale, ¾ mile/1.2km from Blanchland, and 6¼ miles/10km west of Edmundbyers.

Type of walk:
A circular outing that combines moorland hikes and burnside rambles; journeying on way-marked public paths, from country lanes and cart tracks to moorland ways of sandstone and peat.

Park in the free car park/picnic area at the north-west end of the bridge.

Baybridge, favoured by the weekend visitor, provides a tempting start, a restful finish, plus parking, picnic places and tourist information.

From the car park turn left to the corner, by the county boundary, then left again through the gateposts to Newbiggin Hall, signposted and waymarked with yellow arrowheads ("Public Footpath, Riddleham-hope 3 miles"). Initially tree-lined, the lane passes a Wesleyan Providence Chapel (1869), before opening out to walled pastures.

Baybridge is named after the finely-proportioned arched bridge over the infant River Derwent, a river rising from Beldon and Nookton Burns.

Pass between Newbiggin Hall on the left, and a more recent building to the right, before swinging right at the farm steading, and rising on a tree-lined hard-core track to a waymarked gate. Here, by a stone wall, crystal clear water dribbles into a stone drinking trough. At the end of the initial finger of trees, two right forks appear. In both cases continue ahead (roughly west), along a broad, gated track. As mile follows mile and the solitude closes in, the heather-clad flanks of Nookton Fell are particularly pleasing as they rise to the south, above the rock of Castleberry Cleugh and burnside Beldon Shields. Keeping to the central track bearing west and passing Middle Plantation on Beldon Side, look out for a milestone just right of the track.

Positioned roughly at GR925498, the dressed sandstone milestone carries the vertically arranged letters "RIM", an abbreviation of Riddlehamhope, 1 mile/ 1.6km to the west. Further confirmation that this way was a well-used road can be seen in the bedded road stones underfoot.

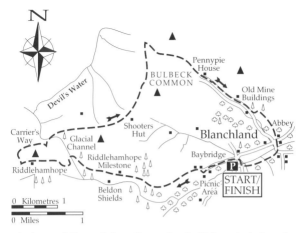

A zigzag falls and rises through a half-forested cleugh above Red Braes prior to passing a rounded cairn on the right to reach the now empty and abandoned buildings of Riddlehamhope, beyond a stiled shelter-belt of venerable pine.

Continue west, soon to pass the final gate (No Bikes) to join the Carrier's Way, a centuries-old route marked by a waymarked stile 200yds/m north-west.

The previous shelter-belt stile provides a seat from which to admire the winding valley of Beldon Burn to the east, in particular, to the walled and pine-topped circular mound on the immediate knowe, possibly an ancient, chieftain's burial mound.

Riddlehamhope, now a sad ruin, was a holding of some standing, as can be seen from its outbuildings and archi-tecture; in particular its square stone chimney stack and the many south-facing windows. "Window Tax", an early form of assessing household tax, held no fears for Riddlehamhope.

Cross the stile on to the open, uncharted heathery acres of Newbiggin Fell, and on a north-east course set sail, by the middle pole of three ahead, for the wind-blown tip of Newbiggin Plantation on the first skyline. Stony sheep traces assist passage, winding through the heather to reach a steep-sided, glaciated horseshoe depression. Descend by a dirt and shale path, pass a rounded sheep stell (a mid-journey stop) to swing left on to a wooden walkway with a waymarked stile. The way continues right, through bracken and heather, to rise north-east then east on to a depression of flattened heather, ascending to an obvious grassy path on the skyline ahead. Here the way widens into a stony, in places rutted, track contouring east to a shooter's stone and tin hut.

Carriers' ways are trans-dales trade routes over which goods were carried in centuries past; mainly by packhorse or later by horse-drawn carts. The ways were much used for transporting lead, using strings of muzzled "galloways" (horses prevented from grazing lead-contaminated grass); each galloway carried graded ore to the smelt mill, or ingots ("pigs") from the mills.

Pass north of the hut, and from the angled fence make for a gate and fence rails ahead to reach two small cairns, one with a drain-pipe, by a second gate. Here beginneth a stretch of great quality where height is gained with ease, spearing north-north-east on grassy, heather-flanked public paths over the open flanks of Birkside Fell and Bulbeck Common. To the left, Devil's Water, to the right and ahead, endless heather-clad ridges. As the flat top of Bulbeck Common is approached, pass through a gated waymarked wall, continuing north on the cairned dirt path for 400yds/m to waymarked crosspaths. Turn right, ascending slightly by yesterday's quarries, before descending with many waymarks to a stiled wall and the crouching farm buildings of Pennypie House.

Pennypie House was a "service-station" alongside this old drove and mine road, that in years past produced and sold pies for a penny.

Pass through the gate and follow the farm lane south-east with the burn, to the houses and Cornish engine house (look, but do not enter) at Shilon. Then, with the waymarked public path, leave the Tarmac for a wooded descent into the striking village of Blanchland.

Blanchland (White Land), is named after the white habits of the Premonstratensian monks, founders of the abbey, who settled by the banks of the Derwent in the mid-1100s, and from 1165 built the abbey, known as Blanchland. The abbey and its surrounds have had a chequered history, fortunately well documented and readily available. The abbot's lodge, guest house and abbey kitchens are now the Lord Crewe Arms, and below a local house evidence was found of silver extraction from lead ore.

From the square, walk south over Blanchland Bridge, turning immediately right past the cottages on to a tree-lined track, alive with birdsong, above the River Derwent, for the return to Baybridge.

WEARDALE

*"The Glory of Weardale is the Moors", wrote Rex Clements
in his Weardale Sketches of 1932. Yet for those who wish
to see, there is more, so much more, to this central North
Pennines dale where all is never as it seems. Indeed, in
"Wardle's" (Weardale's) mother tongue a "dale" is not a
dale, but a strip or division of land. Examples of this are
found in Longdale, by St. John's Chapel, and Turdale, at
Ireshopeburn. Nor is the suffix "hope" ever pronounced
as it is spelt. The "h" remains silent, with the remainder
enunciated as "up" or "op".*

*Weardale's geological character belongs, as do the major-
ity of the Pennines, to the Mountain Limestone period.
Vast beds of shale and sandstone have replaced thinning
bands of limestone below the tops, with such as Killhope
Law, Dead Stones, Burnhope Seat (at 2,447ft/746m, once
the highest in Durham) and Knoutberry Hill capped by
grey millstone or grindstone sill. Such strata, plus an
easterly Ice Age flow, have fashioned today's dale, presenting a narrow jinking valley, enclosed within the slopes
of rippling ridges. The upper levels of limestone mark the
limit of cultivation and habitation. Below, a fine green
sward and an abundance of flowery meadows criss-crossed
by drystone walls greet the walker: above the limestones,
a brown and sombre skyline predominates. Although trees
once covered the entire dale and occasional stands of
conifer are reared today, meadows now abound in which
sheep (mainly Swaledales) and breeding cattle reign supreme.*

*Mountain Limestone strata are endowed with rich veins
of galena – lead ore, often containing small amounts of
copper, zinc and silver. Attractive spars such as barytes,
fluorspar and quartz are also present throughout the
limestone, which has been quarried in large quantities,*

particularly around Stanhope and Frosterley (where it is known as Frosterley Marble).

Access to and through Weardale is good, via the A689, running along the valley floor from Wolsingham to the Durham county boundary at Killhope Cross and on to Nentdale.

North-south passage is less convenient, particularly in winter, with ribbons of Tarmac climbing steeply from Wolsingham, Frosterley, Stanhope, Eastgate, Westgate, St. John's Chapel and Cowshill, into Teesdale, Derwentdale, Rookhopedale and East Allen Dale.

Ten townships, villages and hamlets, of varying size and facilities, line the banks of the winding River Wear and its "up bye" burns. History has conveniently and mysteriously divided the dale into two, "down bye" and "up bye". The elevation of your starting point determines whether you are going up bye or down bye.

Weardale has walks ranging from short strolls to challenging fell and ridge-top treks. Indeed, it is said by a leading Wardle pedestrian "there are more miles of public paths and bridleways in Weardale than in the Great Wall of China."

15 Tunstall Reservoir

As with so many North Pennine walks, this circuit, situated at the predominantly pastoral end of Weardale, offers the walker the entire gamut of farm, forest and fell, in addition to Wolsingham town and Tunstall Reservoir.

Distance:
8 miles/12.8km

Height gain:
699ft/213m

Walking time:
4-4 1/2 hours

Start/Finish:
Wolsingham.
GR077372: on the
A689, 5 1/2 miles/8.8km
west of Crook, and 5 1/2
miles/8.8km east from
Stanhope.

Type of walk:
A scenic circular journey
by Tarmac paths, farm
and woodland tracks,
grass and heather ways,
along a waymarked route
that is never too
demanding.

Parking in the market
place by the town hall and
library.

Wolsingham and its many attractions will delight those who walk its ancient streets. Of special interest is the Church of St. Mary and St. Stephen with its 12th-century tower and floor of Frosterley marble; the Masonic Hall was originally the grammar school, founded in 1612, and only in 1871 ceased using thumbscrews for punishing pupils.

Walk north from the town hall, turning right into Meadhope Street for Angate Square and the bridge over Waskerley Beck. Now on the B6296, Lanchester and Tow Law Road, continue north as far as the junction to the left (signposted to Holywood), prior to the Bay Horse Hotel.

Houses in Meadhope Street, in particular the two dated 1720 and 1740, typify the area, being built of dressed stone or with rubble walls with slate roofs at the front and stone slabs at the back.

Turn left and pass Holywell Farm. Immediately beyond, a waymarked kissing gate on the right leads north by pasture fence and wooded way to the farm steading of Baal Hill House.

"Baal hills" or steads – Roman lead smelters – are common throughout the North Pennines. Piles of stones around a wood fire on the western flank of a suitable hill caught the prevailing wind by means of blast holes or flues between the stones. Fuel came from the nearest wood, which was then named Hag Bank or Hag Hill. Baal Hill House in later centuries housed the bailiff of the Bishops of Durham.

At the farm buildings, swing right (north) along a gated waymarked track for 1¼ pleasing miles (2km), high above Waskerley Beck, by pasture path and Baal Hill Wood to Backstone Beck Farm. From here a farm lane descends sharp left to the dam of Tunstall Reservoir. At the stone gateposts prior to the dam, veer right (north) at an information board, on to a narrow but distinct path that takes the walk onward through Backstone Bank Wood.

Backstone Bank Wood was owned by the Bishops of Durham in the 13th century, who instructed their foresters to preserve "the vert and the venison". Today, the wood is a Site of Special Scientific Interest, with the main interest centring around the 16th-century coppiced oak. By coppicing, life-span and productivity could be doubled.

This woodland section, close by the shoreline, is a delight, particularly in spring and autumn, so it is with some reluctance that the stepped stile at the east end of the vehicular bridge is crossed.

Tunstall Reservoir, now owned by Northumbrian Water, was originally built in 1879 by Weardale and Shildon Waterworks Company. The wet areas by the bridge are unique habitats and support a variety of plants – observe, but do not disturb.

To the east of the stile a gate bears two waymarks; take the right fork, i.e. the wider stony track, to ascend east between dark ranks of conifers. A gated way winds and climbs, overlooked by now-silent worked-out quarries, to reach the open fell. Here, swing left on the Salter's Gate track, rising to the remains of a disused railway depot with signs of the rail-bed running north-west to south-east. At this point turn right, south, with a wallside public path, that steadily ascends Wolsingham North Moor through a series of gates. As the path becomes more distinct and the last wall is left, a triangulation pillar on the left heralds a bracing heather-clad ridge offering far-ranging views south and west of Pikeston Fell and winding Weardale.

As the way descends the fell it is once more restrained by gated walls. Underfoot the ankles are jarred on Thistlewood Lane, as tracks of Tarmac descend south by Thistlewood Farm, Thistlewood House and Thistlewood Hall to reach the B6298. Turn right to the Bay Horse Hotel, then via the outward route for journey's end at the market place.

16 Weatherhill Engine

An exciting and visually pleasing circuit, passing the caves of the Stanhope sprites and our ancestors, in addition to an invigorating promenade along Crawley Edge and the old wagonway of Weatherhill Incline.

Distance:
6¼ miles/10.8km

Height gain:
771ft/235m

Walking time:
4 hours

Start/Finish:
Stanhope. GR995393: astride the A689, 5½ miles/8.8km west from Wolsingham, and 6½ miles/10.4km south of Edmundbyers.

Type of walk:
A circular journey over mixed terrain offering varying experiences, by Stanhope streets, tree-lined burnside paths, cinder railbeds, open fells and quiet lanes.

Parking in the Dales Centre or market place.

Stroll east from the town centre along the main street with the A689, and when brick and stone gives way to green fields, turn left opposite a large filling station, into Woodcroft Gardens. Between the second and third houses on the right a narrow snicket leads east via a stile and waymarks through green pastures to cross Shittlehope Burn footbridge. Turn left and keep to this burnside path, as it winds its waymarked way north for 800yds/m.

This is a delightful passage of colour and birdsong as the burn rumbles by the limestone caverns (known as "cattles" or "cat holes") in the gorge. Linkirk Cave is the largest of these, and provided shelter to early man and a haven for sprites, fairies, and a smuggler or two.

With difficult access and occasional rock falls, the caves and gorge are best seen from a distance, before crossing the footbridge and rising sharp left on a stepped path. Two step stiles appear in quick succession and from the second bear right, diagonally across the pasture, making for a ladder stile. Three more stiled and gated pastures stride wallside west above the rooftops of Stanhope, to emerge on to a cottaged lane rising north.

Turn right with the honeysuckled lane and, as it angles right, leave it to continue north on a narrowing track to a walled and bald plantation. Beyond, a wide stony track leads left (west-north-west), along the flat and heathery rim of Crawley Edge above the grassed-over fanned spoil heaps of Ashes Quarry, a splendid scenic hike of 1 mile/1.6km. Keep to the main cairned track along the rim, ignoring the many pathways dashing left and right, to reach an old wagonway, complete with tunnel, by the site of Crawley Engine, above Crawleyside.

This section tells of the engineering skills and the wheeling and dealing of the railway companies. The Stanhope and Tyne Railway constructed the inclines from 1834, but was declared insolvent in 1840. Taken over by the Stockton and Darlington Railway, of Rocket fame, the inclines were

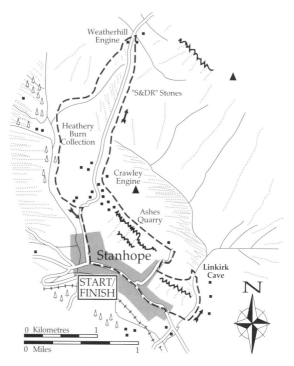

up and running by 1845, hauling limestone and ironstone from Stanhope terminus, up the tunnelled incline by means of the static *Crawley Engine*, and then transferred to the hawsers of the *Weatherhill Winding Engine* for the final ascent.

The now grassy path swings right at the fenced-off entrance to the tunnel, and leads north to the site of Crawley Engine. Its fenced extremities do, however, mark the start of the long incline to Weatherhill, a dirt and cinder track spearing north with the nearby B6278, to reach the crumbling remains of Weatherhill

Engine, an ascent punctuated at intervals by the marker stones (S&DR) of the Stockton and Darlington Railway.

Leave this monument of railway memorabilia and, from the west side of Weatherhill Cottages, one-time railway cottages, trek across the open acres of Weather Hill via a non-too-distinct path to the side of Heathery Burn. This public path tramps the heathery fell heading roughly south-west, before swinging south by the quarry spoil heaps to join an old packhorse trail known as the Velvet Path. Descend west with the waymarked wall past two disused quarries, ideal sites for a refreshment stop, to the mines and quarries alongside Stanhope Burn. Here all may not please the eye, in particular the debris and desolation of a recent fluorspar mine by Heathery Burn confluence.

Walk south with the quarry road, between the burn and the extensive cliffs and black ponds of West Pasture Quarry, desolation that has mellowed over the years as nature reclaims her own.

In 1834, the caves at the meeting of Heathery Burn and Stanhope Burn were quarried. By 1859 the stone beneath the cave system had been removed to reveal the greatest collection of Bronze Age artefacts ever unearthed in Britain, the Heathery Burn Collection.

The south-bound quarry lane, above the tree-lined burn, provides a picturesque return to the road below Crawleyside. Turn right and, with the footpath, drop to Stanhope, where at the foot of Crawleyside Bank, the Grey Bull awaits to refresh those in need.

17 Pawlaw Pike and Five Pikes

A satisfying adventure, sampling en-route endless isolation, secluded green glens, dark, secretive forests and the ghosts of lead mining past.

Distance:
11 miles/17.6km

Height gain:
1,086ft/331m

Walking time:
6 hours

Start/Finish:
Parking area (GR997307) on the B6278, 8 miles/12.8km south of Stanhope, and 5 miles/8km north from Eggleston.

Type of walk:
A circular high-level way traversing moorland paths, at times faint, grassy tracks, needle-strewn forest paths and mine tracks. Never severe, and best walked on a clear day with good companions.

The lonely loop at the head of Sharnberry Gill immediately characterises this walk. Walk north with the B6278 for approximately 100yds/m, turning right beyond the roadside fence to the spoil heaps and mine shafts above. Continue on a distinct heathery track north-north-east, taking the left fork as it clips the eastern end of a line of shooting butts. The path winds its cairned and heathery way, in places squelchy, to the greystone cairns on the eastern shoulder of Long Man.

Long Man is home to clattering grouse, long-legged, disdainful Swaledale sheep and the "Long Man" of Bollihope. Many, many years ago in the fading light of day, two men were seen fighting on the skyline between Teesdale and Weardale. The next morning the body of a very tall stranger was found, and interred beneath the currick on what is now listed on OS maps as Long Man. A four-sided pillar marks the spot. On its eastern side the somewhat indistinct letters "DMCL" date it 1650; on the western side the letters "MM" 2000, remain a mystery.

From this cairned vantage point, the pathway can be seen spearing north-north-east through the wilderness, passing a notice board ("Access for walkers. Vehicles prohibited") below the distinct cone of Pawlaw Pike to the instantly recognisable, cairned ridge of Five Pikes.

A quick dash to Pawlaw (1,601ft/488m) is rewarding, if only to appreciate the sweeping expanse, before heading over Hawkwood Head, via the right fork, to pass below the summit hump of Five Pikes. The trig pillar and nearby triangular cairn, can be reached by a short ascent north from the path.

Although only 1,568ft/478m in height, Five Pikes provides fine views over Weardale, Teesdale and the immediate wilderness of Pikeston Fell and Hamsterley Common.

Return to the pathway, which treks untrammelled for 1¼ miles/2km, with only the cries of curlew, snipe and tumbling peewit for company. Continue on the cairned and posted track to a solitary stand of tortured beech and Scots pine. Swinging half-right with

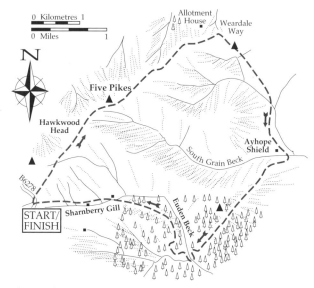

the angled wall to the Weardale Way signs; as the posts draw near note the triangulation pillar of Pikeston Hill on the immediate skyline to the right.

From the gate and wall above Allotment House there are fine views of Frosterley and White Kirkley to the north, small communities that provided "marble" – black lime-stone impregnated with fossils – for many northern churches, including Durham Cathedral.

With the gate behind, plunge south-east on to the heather-clad moor to reach the triangulation pillar. As there is no definite pathway ahead, utilise sheep tracks that snake roughly south-east through the heather for 800yds/m to join a vehicle track. Swing right with this dirt-rutted track, descending roughly south to the hidden confluence of Steel Burn and North Grain

Beck. Once across North Grain Beck the path climbs slightly, still following the true right bank, to above the tree line. Continue south, over a makeshift stile, by a crumbling wall and hawthorn line, to the fallen stones of Ayhope Shield, above The Meeting of the Grains. In addition to the pleasing views down Ayhope Beck to Hamsterley Forest, note the pathway rising south-west from South Grain Beck over the flanks of Brown Law and Black Hill.

Once across the beck the narrow grass and dirt path ascends south-west over Hamsterley Common for about 1 mile/1.75km to the forest edges below Black Hill. After its initial windings, this thin but assured path continues its cairned way. A wall gate allows entry into a blanket of spruce, and by a purple waymark post turn left on to a dirt track, then immediately swing right into a narrow waymarked tube leading south-west. Underfoot a grass and pine-needle path descends silently to the end of the tunnel; ignore all the incoming rides and paths for ³/₄ mile/1.25km until the fork in a harvested stand.

Bear left to a wide road below, and cross to a waymarked path zigzagging steeply between sitka to the banks of musical Euden Beck flowing in from the west. Once across the beck, turn left for 150yds/m to join one of the main haul roads sweeping down from the right. Rise right (west-north-west), with this road as it sharply ascends to Sharnberry Flat. Ignore any lefts or rights until a small concrete water tank/reservoir is met. At this point leave the wide way and continue west on a track through the coniferous corridor for 800yds/m to the forest boundary stile above Sharnberry Beck.

For 1¹/₄ miles/2km west, the stony road rises through the gill before a sandstone overhang on the left signals the return to the parking place and B6278.

18 Eastgate and Rookhope

Rookhope provides all things to all walkers – botanists, geologists, historians (social and industrial), artists, poets, photographers and writers all find inspiration in the wooded denes, the floral meadows, and the mines and quarries of yesterday that pepper the folding fells.

Distance:
8 1/4 miles/13.2km

Height gain:
1,099ft/335m

Walking time:
4-4 1/2 hours

Start/Finish:
Eastgate. GR953388: astride the A689 and Rookhope Burn, 4 1/4 miles/6.8km west of Stanhope.

Type of walk:
This contrasting journey of high interest is rarely demanding. Walking is through floral denes on to flat-topped fells, on farm tracks, burnside paths, country lanes, long-gone wagonways and disused railbeds.

Limited parking by the church and hall.

Shy and half-hidden Eastgate, snuggling alongside Rookhope Burn, provides the starting point for this intriguing walk. Walk north, from the church and village hall crossroads to Holm House, ascending the hedge-bound lane that guides the Weardale Way.

Eastgate marked the eastern gate into the medieval hunting forest (Bishop's Park) of the Bishops of Durham. It is a village which would have suited that enthusiastic pedestrian and writer of the mid-1900s, S.P.B. Mais, who explained in This Unknown Island *that he "made a bee-line in every village for the church for a quick glimpse of ancient history, and the pub for more leisurely study of modern history". The church dates from 1888; the Cross Keys Inn, its roof pegged with sheeps' bones, is 300 years older.*

Holm House and adjacent signpost ("Rookhope 2½ miles"), the yard awash with multi-coloured cockerels, frees the roots from its timbered shackles, allowing the way to continue to picturesque Hole House. Here it forks right, into a small copse of holly, beech, hazel and dog rose. In places paved and cobbled, the way wanders north by Ambling Gate Bank alongside the water-worn stones of Rookhope Burn, passing hidden remains of kilns, quarries and mines, before crossing Rookhope Burn by a footbridge leading right by a step stile on to the Eastgate-Rookhope road.

It is barely a mile/1.6km to the ribboned streets of Rookhope, via Stotfield Burn. Chapel Row, with its Wesleyan Methodist Chapel of 1863, heralds the houses of Rookhope and leads to the post office, with its redundant flower-bedecked petrol pump, at a Z-bend. Directly opposite, a Lead Mining Trail sign indicates the path to Boltslaw Incline.

This wagonway, the Boltslaw Incline, hauled limestone and ganister from Rookhope to Redgate Head, for trans-shipment to Parkhead (known as Blanchland Station) above Stanhope. The Incline, born in the mid-1800s and died in the 1920s, handled hawser-drawn wagons by means of two steam-driven winding engines. Remains of both buildings can be seen today. The hawsers were kept in line by, and ran over, wide rollers placed at regular intervals, positioned horizontally on the straights and vertically on the curves. Photographs in Rookhope show the devastation caused by a runaway train of wagons.

Take a stony track ascending by a row of cottages and, keeping left at a fork, pass through a five-bar gate to join the lower section of the wagonway bed. This mile/1.6km long track, with a left-hand sweep, rises 574ft/175m to the silhouetted remains of the engine winding house and shops bisecting Longshaw End and Redgate Head. Note the remains of the first engine house, with its worn stones, the central stone foundations for the hawser rollers, the occasional rotting wooden sleeper and the regular sleeper depressions, plus the scatter of galena and fluorspar samples. Wander round the engine house and surrounds, then walk north to view the endless fells surrounding Bolt's Law (1,773ft/540m), across which chugged the standard gauge rolling stock of the Weardale Iron Company, the highest line in England. Return to Rookhope.

Rookhope (1,200ft/366m above sea level) originated from the Gallic "roe", a mass of stones, and the Celtic "hwpp", sheltered valley. In the 12th century "crawcoals" (soft coal) and iron were worked. "Clay-cats", coal mixed with clay, were also produced.

An undated charter of Bishop Pudsey of Durham (1153-96), decreed that "dogs in Rookhope should not have a foot amputated, but that the shepherd should lead them on leashes so that they may protect their cattle from wolves."

In 1569, there was the Rookhope Raid, when Tyneside reivers stole 600 head of Rookhopedale's sheep and nowt

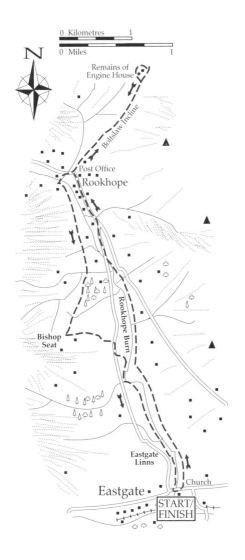

0 Kilometres 1

0 Miles 1

N

Remains of
Engine House

Bolts Law Incline

Post Office
Rookhope

Rookhope Burn

Bishop
Seat

Eastgate
Linns

Eastgate

Church

START/
FINISH

(cattle), only to meet their match when pursued by Weardale men, recorded in 1792, in the ballad "Rookhope Ryde":

> *"Rookhope stands in a pleasant place,*
> *If the false thieves wad let it be;*
> *But away they steal our goods apace,*
> *And ever an ill death may they dee!"*

Beyond the whitewashed walls of Rookhope Inn, a minor crossroads carries twin bridleway signs. Take the left turn and cross Rookhope Burn by the wooden walkway to face a confusion of waymarks, signposts and tracks at an industrial building. Take the main dirt track left, south-south-east, with the building to the right. Initially over sterile spoil, the way follows a disused rail line that ran to Height's Limestone Quarry above Westgate, ascending south-south-west past Smailsburn Farm to reach the derelict cottage of Bishop Seat.

Turn left by the ruined house, to a gated stone wall, from where a public path descends to Hanging Wells Farm and the Eastgate road. Swing right on to the road and left at the first field gate, descending south-east with a tree-lined gill to join the thin path on the true right bank of Rookhope Burn, another change of landscape for the final 1¼ miles/2km burnside ramble to Eastgate. This delightful burnside journey, with Weardale's woodland and waterside wildlife, climaxes with a succession of four half-hidden musical linns: Holm Linn, Middle Linn by The Washpool, Dunter Linn and, finally, Low Linn. Below, the pathway, alongside a discreetly-placed caravan park, swings left over a footbridge and climbs a few steps to the crossroads by the church.

19 Wearhead and St. John's

An explosion of colour, birdsong and ever-changing views greet the walker as every corner is turned and every rise conquered. This is a journey with a tale to tell, pleasing to the eye and easy on the feet, but can be wet underfoot along Sedling Rake after prolonged periods of rain.

Distance:
6 1/4 miles/10.8km

Height gain:
886ft/270m

Walking time:
3-4 hours

Start/Finish:
Wearhead. GR854395: straddles the A689 9 miles/14.4km west from Stanhope, and 1 mile/1.6km south of Cowshill.

Type of walk:
Circular and never demanding, this scenically varied walk crams a great deal of "up bye" Weardale into its mine and quarry roads, drovers' tracks and flower-laden riverside pastures.

Limited off-road parking. Please avoid blocking local access.

Wearhead, where the historic River Wear rises from the meeting of the waters of Killhope, Wellhope and Burnhope, marks the start of this fine fell and riverside walk. Walk north from the post office, for a short distance up Front Street, turning right at a public bridleway sign beyond the family butcher's shop of Mr Humble. Continue, rising north-east, by wicket gate and stile by Sparks House, on to a dirt and grass track ascending the mine and quarry-ravaged flanks of Bail Hill.

Keep to the left path at each of the three forks, as the way climbs between grass, thyme and buttercup-clad spoil heaps to a gated and stiled wall on the skyline ahead, a point from which to enjoy fine views over the chimney pots of Wearhead. From the stile, a narrow trace leads north-east to a waymarked stile by the corner of a white house. Turn right on to a lane, and after 50yds/m, left on to a farm track (signposted to Newfield Sedling). The track travels north, passing Halliwell House, and follows a wall on the right, before emerging on to West Blackdene Pasture ascending, via a thin grassy path, to the walled and gated crossroads of Sedling Vein and Rake.

The nearby, one-time rich, vein is now but a gouged and pitted scar, though worth a careful visit, as it may yield an interesting crystal. It certainly provides dramatic sightings of the pock-marked remains of Burtree Pastures Mine and Midge Pits Vein.

From the crossroads turn right, and with the grass track of Sedling Rake, in places wet and rutted, walk east by Race Head for an invigorating mile/1.6km of scenic delights.

Mile upon mile of "up bye" Weardale, from the dark heights of its outer rim to the softer green pastures in the valley below, is revealed along this old green road, a trail much-favoured long ago by drovers, cadgers and miners.

At the road junction, by a conifer stand indicating

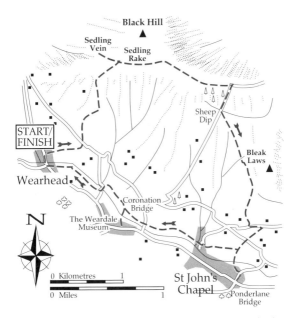

"Lead Mining Trail" to the west, turn right with the road. After 150yds/m, by a sheep dip and pens, turn left on to a wide green road descending south-east over the flanks of Bleak Laws. The continuing journey, with the ever-present Swaledale and in the company of curlew and peewit, runs between steep stone walls over Carr Brow Pastures to a lane above St. John's Chapel. How pleasing it is to gaze down on the tall narrow houses of St. John's and watch the motorised world whizz by.

Turn left for a few strides, to join the Weardale Way as it veers right on its stepped and stiled waymarked way to the northern banks of the River Wear.

A visit, via Ponderlane footbridge, to the market town of St. John's Chapel, locally abbreviated to St. John's, even if only for an ice cream, is worthwhile. "Chapel" (1865), town hall, pubs and mart, all cluster round its paved square. The "chapel" or church dedicated to St. John the Baptist, from which St. John's Chapel derives its name, was separated from Stanhope Parish in 1866.

Back to the Weardale Way, walk west through six stiled and gated walls. Pass the house by the sixth wall on its north side, on to a picturesque path leading to Wearhead, a waymarked riverside walk by tumbling linn and flower-lined bank that, in its way, equals the many delights of its much-vaunted neighbour. At Coronation Bridge, by Ireshopeburn, learn a little more of the dale by turning left to pass Wesley's Thorn and visit the Weardale Museum of High House Chapel.

Ireshopeburn, pronounced locally as "Ice-up", is a gangly village with three bridges. The foundation stone of Coronation Bridge, laid on 20 June 1837, commemorates the coronation of Queen Victoria. At its southern end stands "Wesley's Thorn", a bush marking the spot where the Reverend John Wesley (1703-1791), preached to the miners and farmers of Ireshopeburn during his visits to Weardale. The present bush carries a preservation order.

From the New House end of Coronation Bridge, continue the Weardale journey west, the final stretch to Wearhead a walk of charm and peace. Try to ignore the redundant and part-dismantled fluorspar plant on the right, before reaching, via a sun-dappled avenue of trees, the colourful cottages of West Blackdene. Here the bridge is crossed to the south bank of the Wear, and the Way swings right by Waterside Farm to reach journey's end at Wearhead's new road bridge.

20 Puddingthorn Edge

*Tumbling burns, white lands and black lands domi-
nate the dished corrie of upper Weardale, for gone
are the flowering pastures and the ranks of drystone
walls. All is now endless fell. This walk provides a
stone chair from which to survey the majesty of
this dale on the grand circle of Puddingthorn Edge.*

Distance:
5 1/2 miles/8.8km

Height gain:
771ft/235m

Walking time:
3 1/2 hours

Start/Finish:
Cowshill. GR856406:
on the A689,
1 mile/1.6km north of
Wearhead, and 3 3/4
miles/6km south of
Allenheads.

Type of walk:
*A burnside and fellside
circular walk that extols
the majestic isolation of
Upper Weardale, first on
waymarked burnside
paths, then by a green
road ascending to thin
heathery trods, finally
descending by a carriers'
way to the bosom of the
dale. A walk for a clear
day.*

Public car park and inn.

Cowshill, the Kathmandu of "up bye" Weardale,
provides the starting point of this short scenic walk.

Walk west on the waymarked Weardale Way, from

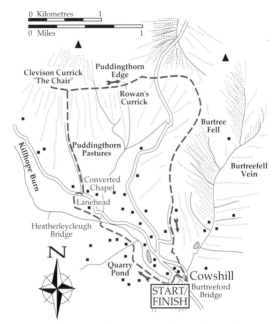

Burtreeford Bridge below Cowshill, along the west bank of Killhope Burn.

Cowshill, an old name denoting open pastures, is a village community adjoining a forest. Burtreeford Bridge, built 1839, straddles the ravine into which an attractive waterfall of Killhope Burn plunges. The great fault in the limestone exposed just above the falls is universally known as "Burtreeford Dyke".

Continue for 1¹/₄ miles/2km by the slabbed and stepped burn, by gate, stile and stone cottage to the bridge at Heatherycleugh. Cross to the north bank and, with the waymarks, turn left as far as the third wall, swinging right and ascending with the wall to Burnt Hills. Here a wide stony track north, joins the A689 at Lanehead. Walk right, and at the converted chapel, turn left to rise north with the walled green road over Puddingthorn Pastures.

The Primitive Methodist Chapel, erected 1831 and rebuilt in the 1850s, has been converted into a private house, as have many other places of worship in the North Pennines.

Clevison Currick can now be seen standing proud on the western shoulder of Puddingthorn Edge as the green road passes through a gate and continues its grassy way.

Green roads, lifelines from dale to dale, of which there are many examples in Weardale, are relics dating from times when trade was conducted by foot and by wagon. Ways, between two walls 10 paces apart, provide today's pedestrian with many fine walks.

On High Puddingthorn the flower-carpeted green road finally leaves the restraining walls and bursts on to the open, heathery, flat fell. A twin trod sweeps north over grass and heather to the dark rim of Puddingthorn Edge and the stones of Clevison Currick.

Extensive inquiry failed to provide any information on Clevison Currick. What did emerge was that the currick is known locally as "The Chair", as it is in the style of a large armchair complete with stone seat.

The fine views can now be enjoyed, if not in comfort, at least at leisure; in particular, the entire rim of outer Weardale, and below, the green pastures and picturesque villages.

Leave "The Chair" by a thin track snaking east through heather, making for Rowan's Currick. Although marked on the OS map, it is a sad, small pile of stones with just a hint of a circular base. At the stone pile swing left making for the left end of the shooting butts in the cleugh ahead. From there revert to a thin eastbound path, over the rather damp moor, to a wicket gate in the angled county boundary wall. Through the gate, follow a fence to the Allenheads-Cowshill road.

Cross the road and, by the metal gate, rise over Allenheads Common, beside a wall, to a waymarked gate leading south over Burtree Fell. The final 1³/₄ miles/2.8km to Cowshill, over a carriers' way, is a delightful descent, presenting a plethora of fine vistas and interesting insights into 19th-century lead mines below, as Burtree Fell and the houses of Cogley and Holyhead are passed on the return to Cowshill.

In the depths of the 19th- and early 20th-century North Pennine winters, miners and farmers travelled to their work on large wooden skates. Known as "skees", these 6 feet long and 6 inches wide platforms were used in the fashion of today's Nordic cross country skiers. A six feet pole, or "skee pleeat", was used with the skees, "for steering and for leaping over walls etc".

Such activities eventually became the chief sport in the Dales, with barrels of ale being awarded as prizes at Cowshill. One can imagine the miners at Burtree Pasture competing, for the mine broke many records, including the staggering output in 1909 of 10,000 bings (a "bing" was 896lbs/407kilos) of lead ore.

21 Sedling Vein and Fell

This is a varied walk, with evocative reminders of a lead mining past. Constant changes in scenery and mood add to the items of industrial, social and physical history on the way.

Distance:
5¾ miles/9.2km

Height gain:
856ft/261m

Walking time:
3 hours

Start:
Cowshill Car Park.
GR856406:

Finish:
Allenheads.

Type of walk:
A linear high-level hike by carriers' ways, grassy paths and the Weardale Way to Allenheads.

Walking north, follow the roadside signpost ("Lead Mining Trail. Public Footpath"), through the car park to the notice ("Private Property Keep Out") at a chained gate. Notice and padlock apply to wheeled visitors only, with passage for walkers available at the side of the gateposts. Continue along the track, flanked by the rusting and rotting remains of yesterday's mines.

So powerful are the ghosts within this moonscape, that little imagination is needed to reincarnate the sounds and smells of man and beast struggling to prise lead from the heart of the North Pennines. Do resist any temptation to explore shafts and mine entrances – they are extremely dangerous.

Swing right, ascending at the first fork for a U-turn through the gate on to a mine track ascending east above the gully of Sedling Vein.

This deep hush and its spoil heaps are today softened by grass cover, although bare sterile patches still remain at higher levels. Here the geologist and the curious can search for discarded minerals – coloured crystals bearing such names as Blue John, Paper Spar, Dog Tooth and Derbyshire Spar.

The gated track beyond Sedling Vein follows Sedling Rake east, a well-defined way though damp in places. At the double gates, an old wall staggers down from Black Hill. Turn sharp left with the dyke to ascend the hill, with its crumbling stone shelter. Pause to view the dappled folds of Weardale before descending north-west with the fallen stones to a public path alongside wall and fence. Turn right (north), with the fence past shooting butts, to join a section of wall, north-north-west to its right angle and adjoining slip rail. Pass through, contouring north-west over the open acres of Sedling Fell, above Burtree (local name for elder) Pasture Vein and Mine, by lonely Coptcleugh.

Burtree Pasture Mine was the deepest mine in upper Weardale, its shaft, sunk through Firestone to the Jew Limestone, penetrates some 1,800ft/547m.

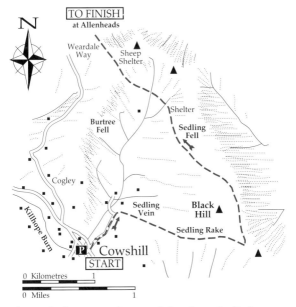

The path shown on the map is in places indistinct on the ground, but the route is easily maintained by keeping the first sheep shelter and shieling on the left. As several small sykes are crossed, swing north-west, making for a prominent semi-circular sheep shelter on the skyline ahead. A distinct path, via a crumbling shieling, leads to the waymarked Weardale Way over Allendale Common.

Walk west with the wall, through the iron gate, to join the B6295, descending by Bulman's Bridge and Allen Cleugh for 1¹/₂ miles/2.4km to the half-hidden hamlet of Allenheads, a road walk that is eased underfoot by narrow grass verges, and overhead by the ever-widening pastoral views of East Allen Dale.

22 Killhope Law

This journey to the dark side of three counties is for the curious, the adventurous, skilled navigators, and those strong of wind and limb with a propensity for brock-hopping. En route there are extensive and intriguing views, invigorating solitude, and many species of upland flora and fauna.

Distance:
6 miles/9.6km

Height gain:
666ft/203m

Walking time:
3 1/2 hours

Start/Finish:
Killhope Lead Mining Centre. GR825432: by Killhope Burn and the A689, 2 miles/3.2km north-west of Cowshill, and 3 miles/4.8km east from Nenthead.

Type of walk:
Part of the Weardale Way waymarked track, through forest and fell, part grassy roadside verges, and part naked peat to and from the county abutment of Durham, Northumberland and Cumbria.

Not advised in poor visibility.

The attractions of the Killhope Lead Mining Centre, a World Heritage Site, makes this an ideal place to start. This restored site of Park Level Mine and Crushing Mill is a lasting memorial and charismatic reminder of man's efforts to wrest lead ore from the heart of the North Pennines, from Roman times to the industry's final decline in the early 1900s. Visit the Centre, for Killhope was one of the productive jewels in Blackett's and Beaumont's Weardale mining crown. Learn about gins, hushes, trammers, bouse, deads, hotching and dolly tubs, buddles, jiggers, the massive 33ft/10m water wheel and the working conditions endured by the washer boys of Killhope, long hours in cruel wet surroundings, recorded in a local song:–

*"It's early in the morning we rise at five o'clock,
And the little lads come to the floor to knock, knock, knock.
So come my little washer boys, come, let's away,
We're bound down to slavery for fourpence a day."*

From the Lead Mining Centre, cross the A689 road to enter the forest track (signposted "Weardale Way, Public Footpath Carriers' Way: 1^1/$_2$ miles") winding over Carriers' Hill, a quiet, gated way north over High Linn, scarred by dead and dying stumps, to the open heathery fell of Great Hill. Continue ascending north, initially alongside a rush-ridden sike well marked with posts, before higher ground provides drier conditions underfoot. The thin path swings right as the barely noticeable col carrying the Durham/Northumberland boundary is passed. Now descending, the way offers fine views north of the green acres of East Allen Dale beyond the horseshoe reservoirs of Dodd and Byerhope.

As lead production increased, and bigger machines demanded more power, water was gathered from every stream in the catchment area and channelled into reservoirs, thus ensuring a constant and steady supply for the giant water wheels that drove the plant and mills of Allenheads and Allen Dale. The water from higher reservoirs frequently fed those at lower levels in addition to powering local machinery.

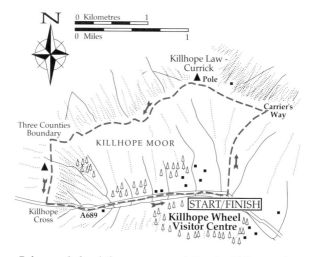

Below and ahead the grass covered Carriers' Way can be seen descending to Allenheads, a route used by the ore carriers, men with teams of hardy dales packponies yoked in groups of up to twenty-five. Later, when roads were improved, two-wheeled carts hauled by larger horses were used. Thus was the dressed lead ore transported from the Killhope mines to the smelt mills at Allenheads and Allendale Town up to 1883.

With the silence of the fells broken only by the cheerful song and persistent cry of lark and curlew, a small pile of stones is met marking a stony track rising left (west), to a solitary decaying hut. Beyond, a fell path indicates the final strides to the adorned peak of Killhope Law (2,208ft/673m), bearing a hive-shaped currick, a triangulation pillar and an impressive lone pine pole of great height.

Bog-hoppers, as they follow the zigzag boundary line

of rotting posts south-west and west for 1¼ miles/2km, will be agog with excitement; lesser mortals, not so. For ahead lies a continuum of sodden, dark peat brocks, best negotiated for the first 800yds/m from Killhope Law alongside the occasional fence post with distant Cross Fell as a marker. Thereafter, the way wobbles west-south-west over the watershed above West Allen Dale and Weardale, making for an incongruous pile of stones and a duo of fire beaters, strange indicators for this dark assemblage of three counties. Once this common ground is reached, conditions underfoot improve somewhat.

Swing left from the junction, with rotting or uprooted posts, descend south on a faint trace to a complete fence by a "Cumberland 1868", boundary stone. It is but a short descent south to Killhope Cross and the A689, at 2,056ft/627m, the highest A-road in England.

Killhope Cross, a medieval boundary cross embedded in stone, marked the extremity of the county of the Prince Bishops. Originally placed at the joining of Durham, Northumberland and Cumberland, it has since been moved, it is not known when, to the roadside of the high pass.

From this lofty pass walk east, descending on the wide grass roadside verge, via Killhope Bank and Killhopehead Bridge for 1¼ miles/2.4km to journey's end at Killhope Lead Mining Centre.

23 Dead Stones and Burnhope Seat

A circular journey of glorious isolation, which in clear dry conditions, provides an unforgettable day on the hills. Much of the route, although not a public path, follows the county and district boundary, a way hallowed for generations. The present farmer, whose boundaries march with the high circuit, welcomes considerate walkers, but please keep to the prescribed route.

Distance:
16 miles/25.6km

Height gain:
1,611ft/491m

Walking time:
8 hours

Start/Finish:
Cowshill. GR856406: on the A689, 4 miles/6.4km south of Allenheads, and 6 miles/9.6km east from Nenthead.

Type of walk:
A serious walk around the edge of upper Weardale, traversing grass paths, roadside verges, miners' tracks and ill-defined trods that stutter through a desert of peat on the summit ridges.

Walk west, from the south end of Burtreeford Bridge below Cowshill, following the waymarked Weardale

Way west along the flower-strewn banks of tumbling Killhope Burn. Pass a watery quarry, below Cowshill, via stile/gate to Low Waller's Cottage and Heatherycleugh.

Cowshill is a focal point for walkers, wildlife enthusiasts and a mecca for geologists. Named after the hamlet of Burtreeford, the noted basaltic Burtreeford Dyke, said to contain around twenty configurations of strata, runs south into Teesdale and north into East Allen Dale. Vertical standing whinstone, shot from an erupting interior, can be seen in the bed of Killhope Burn below the quarry.

Cross Heatherycleugh Bridge to the north bank of Killhope Burn and continue west to Killhopeburn Bridge. Here the Weardale Way leaves the burn to ascend north over pastures (beware the quarry rim) to join the roadside verges of the A689, a road that rises 502ft/153m in 2¾ miles/4.5km, passing Killhope Lead Mining Centre en route to Killhope Cross.

Killhope Lead Mining Centre is a required stop, where the lot of a lead miner can be experienced. Lead from Killhope mines was used in pipes, water cisterns, lead shot, roof flashing, paint manufacture and pewter; centuries earlier, church roofs and walls were clad with lead sheets. North from the road stands Holy Well, a 19th-century miner-farmer's smallholding. In the 1870s, on Weardale's western rim, lead supported in excess of 1,000 souls; today's population is barely 100.

Killhope Cross, a small stone cross on the county boundary, is said to have marked the boundaries of Northumberland, Durham and Cumberland. Many such medieval crosses marked the boundaries of the See of Durham, e.g. on Nag's Head.

From Killhope Cross, the lay-by stile leads south by wall and fence, ascending to the barren wastes of Knoutberry Hill, beyond which, to the south-west, stands Nag's Head, reached on a thin trod by fence and wall.

An interesting diversion can be made as the summit wall is met, by taking 150 paces north-north-west over the tussocky fell to discover a clutch of medieval crosses similar to Killhope Cross. One complete cross and two stumps are embedded in a triangular base stone, and several partially buried stones or crosses surround the base. Could they be the "Eades Stones", placed by King Eadred to mark the Palatinate of the Prince Bishops?

To the south, via a grass path and county fence, the silhouetted stones on the summit of Dead Stones beckon.

Dead Stones, complete with tall, pointed cairn, shelter cairns and a fine stone bothy (by masons unknown), is also a place to rest and refresh, to contemplate the dales and the endless rippling ridges that grace these lonely North Pennines. Gaze east over the catchment of Burnhope and note the walls of "The Malekoff and Redan" built during the Crimean War to commemorate the battles of those names.

A narrow path, continually looking for dry land, is followed south to Burnhope Head and Burnhope Seat. At 2,447ft/746m, the highest point on the walk lies in Cumbria, while the nearby triangulation point is in Durham. Note also, by the fence junction, an estate boundary stone – "H" on its west side, "E" on the east side.

Continue south-east with the fence to Scraith Head, a slithery stretch that earns the epithet "Politicians'

Way" – one step forward, two steps back, three steps left, four steps right, and finally a U-turn!

Such antics allow close and complete scrutiny of the ground, which is covered with cloudberry, known locally as "knoutberry", that produces orange-red fruits with a delightful flavour. Note also, where the county boundary fence turns right, a dressed stone boundary marker (in two halves), engraved on its north side "1880", east "GH", south "EC", and west "DC", marking disputed estate boundaries settled in court, circa 1880. "EC" stood

Ecclesiastical Commissioners, the largest landowners in Weardale.

From the old boundary marker go forth, south-east, into the wilderness, assisted by an intermittent line of stunted rotting fence posts marking the district boundary of Weardale and Teesdale, initially for 800yds/m to the cairned knowe (2,356ft/718m) above Redgleam Quarry. The next destination, the twin domes and currick of Scaud Hill, requires a short but squelchy trek of ∫ mile/1.2km, east-north-east. Finally, with bog-hopping skills honed over the last few miles, the haul east-south-east with the disadvantaged fence over Langtae Head, to the white triangulation point (2,323ft/708m) on the cairn-strewn tops above High Field, is easily achieved.

Leave this stony hill, and its old mines, by marker stone and narrow path, descending east to the wide track traversing Coldberry End. Turn left on to this causeway leading to the floor of Weardale, a way that not only eases passage but presents, arguably, the most complete yet seldom-seen panorama of upper Weardale. Proceed by stony track and gated Tarmac lane, east of the shelter trees of Burnhope Reservoir, to an old lime kiln and the road left to the reservoir dam.

Burnhope Reservoir, built in the 1930s, covers what was the village of Burnhope, including its old packhorse bridge. Today, linear walkways tread its north and south tree-lined banks.

The final picturesque mile to Cowshill winds north from the dam, by a quiet walled lane, passing Blackcleugh Farm (start/finish if staying at Blackcleugh Camping Barn) for a well deserved rest and refreshment.

TEESDALE

This colourful dale has inspired the pens and palettes of writers and artists of genius: Scott, Dickens, Wainwright, Turner and Cotman have all extolled its splendours. For this scenic and scientific gem we have two natural phenomena to thank. Firstly, the laying down of the earth's crust from the beginning of time, and more recently, the work of the Ice Age. As the earth evolved, the area was submerged under water, at the bottom of which settlings eventually formed to become shale, sandstone and limestone. Later, molten rock was squeezed between the layers and faults of these sedimentary rocks. In what is now Teesdale the fluid rock, on cooling, formed a hard stone called Whin Sill, and tremendous heat crystallised the base layers of limestone into a crumbly rock known as Sugar Limestone.

When the Ice Age came, scouring the terrain, the resilient Whin Sill and limestone were left protruding through the clay deposits; Cronkley Fell and Widdybank Fell are classic examples of this.

The results of this frenzied activity are highlighted by the sweeps and surges of the River Tees, whose seasonal spates are now controlled by the Cow Green Reservoir. From Tees Head, high on Cross Fell, the river pounds and pummels the steps and drops of Whin Sill at Cauldron Snout, High Force and Low Force.

On the high fells, the Sugar Limestone crumbles and neutralises the acid soils to provide a fertile bed for the many arctic and alpine plants found there, a feature known as the "Teesdale Assemblage". Here geology, geography, climate and isolation have produced an unequalled habitat for the flora and fauna of Teesdale, now within the North Pennines Area of Outstanding Natural Beauty. As a result all visitors must observe the country code in general and the rules and requests governing the dale in particular.

Access into this broad and rolling dale is easy from the south or east, but from the west and north it is not so convenient. Four roads funnel west from the wide mouth of the dale; one winds north to Weardale leaving three to home-in on Middleton-in-Teesdale. To Lunedale and Baldersdale minor roads provide pleasing short journeys while the B6278 from Eggleston to Stanhope and Weardale has sweeping moorland views but endless inclines. Two steep ribbons of Tarmac remain, exiting north from Newbiggin and Langdon Beck, climbing to 1,990ft/607m and 2,057ft/627m respectively, before careering north into Weardale.

From Barnard Castle west to Langdon Beck there are two towns; the substantial market town of Barnard Castle and the smaller Middleton-in-Teesdale, capital of upper Teesdale, along with eight charming villages, that diminish in size as the dale's head is approached.

The wide variation, to suit all abilities, should enable walkers to enjoy a taste of Teesdale and perhaps go just that little bit further.

24 The Greta and the Tees

A walk of great charm, by tree-lined river bank and silver stream, whose delights are encapsulated in Rokeby *by Sir Walter Scott:*

> *"O Brignall Banks are wild and fair,*
> *And Greta Woods are green."*

There is much to attract the naturalist along the way, for Teesdale is a flowering dale, overflowing with birdlife. Time should also be allowed for exploring Barnard Castle.

Distance:
11 1/4 miles/18km

Height gain:
623ft/190m

Walking time:
6 hours

Start/Finish:
Greta Bridge.
GR086132: by the A66(T), 4 1/2 miles/7.2km south-east from Barnard Castle.

Type of walk:
A longish riverside circuit, alongside the Tees and its tributary the winsome Greta. A marked way by pasture path and waterside woodland tracks, in places overgrown and eroded, country lanes and prepared riverside walks.

Parking is a few hundred yds/m north-west, beyond the Morritt Arms Hotel.

Greta Bridge, now removed from the busy A66, provides a quiet and peaceful start for this tranquil walk. A yard or so west of the graceful arch of Greta Bridge, a public footpath marker leads over a stepped wall into a pasture flanking the true left bank of the River Greta. The river is abandoned by the rising path, which follows a wooded boundary fence, first south and then west, eventually descending on a distinct pathway to the half-hidden ruin of St. Mary's Church, below the hamlet of Brignall.

St. Mary's stands close by the site of the medieval village of Brignall, south of and lower than the present village. Its ramshackle churchyard contains many leaning and crumbling tombstones, dating from the mid-1600s to the late-1800s, and two opened tombs.

West of the church the field path leads over a marked stile into Tebb Wood, with the boulder-strewn bed of the River Greta now immediately left. As the timber thins, an open area is met and passage west is assisted by a waymarked tree trunk. Ahead, the heavy tree cover on Brignall Banks can be seen, and is entered through a patch of newly-planted broadleaves by means of a rail stile.

The path on this lengthy stretch along an ever-narrowing gully, in addition to frequent ups and downs, squirms through thick undergrowth, or disappears beneath one's feet due to land slips. Sir Walter Scott got it right – "O Brignall Banks are wild". Note also Edward Whymper's advice "Heed well the placement of the feet": take great care through Brignall Banks.

On emerging below Moor House Farm, descend left, over a cattle grid, to the renovated Brignall Mill. Here waymarks indicate the route to the riverside. Swing right, ascend a few stone steps, then cross the foot-

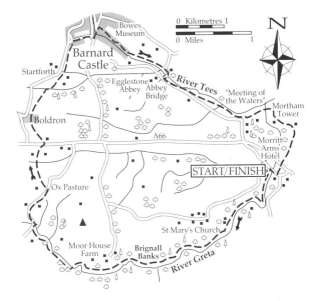

bridge to the true right bank of the Greta. Turn right and, with river, pathway and one more footbridge, over Thwaite Beck, walk north-west for one very pleasant mile to Rutherford Bridge.

From the bridge walk north with the road for 800yds/m, to pass Ox Pasture Farm on the left. As the road rises beyond, turn left on to a cart track running west. Cross a cattle grid and continue to the end of the fence. Here, swing right, up a field to a stile in the wall ahead. Proceed north, with Kilmond Scars stretching west on the left hand, passing through two gates, to Kilmond Wood Farm.

Walk through the steading to the A66(T), a thunder-ing road that requires a swift but careful crossing to its north side and a lane entrance with a public bridleway signpost. Over the stile two pastures lead north-west to a tree-planted pathway heading to the church in Boldron village.

Cross the village road and turn right for about 100yds/m to a public path post by a black gate. Cross the stile for a hurdling hike north, over a miscellany of waymarked stiles, through seven pastures and the narrowest of stone footbridges, to reach the Startforth road. Descend to Hall Farm and take the first right into Startforth, passing Morris Memorial School and the immaculate Church of the Holy Trinity. Once past, turn left through a kissing gate on to a gravelled path descending to a roadway, that is crossed prior to the girdered-metal footbridge over the sweeping Tees.

Barnard Castle ("Barney" to Dalesmen), stands at the mouth of Teesdale, a small market town with a big history. The castle above County Bridge (1569) was built in the 1100s by Bernard Balliol, whose descendant, John Balliol, founded Balliol College, Oxford as a penance for assaulting a bishop.

Above Demesnes, towers the impressive Bowes Museum, a French-style chateau, packed with art treasures and collections of international importance amassed, in 15 years from 1860, by John and Josephine Bowes, son and daughter-in-law of an Earl of Strathmore. There is much more of interest in Barney; more than can be crammed into one day.

Pass the 19th-century woollen factory of Mill Court and rise into the town, turning right at Grey Lane to Demesnes Fields. Here a wide track, waymarked Abbey Bridge, continues through the playing fields to the converted Demesnes Mill. The sedate waters of the Tees, a contrast with Walks 28 and 31, lead for a gentle 1 1/4 miles/2km to the high and castellated Abbey Bridge.

Prior to the farm, gaze over the river to the silhouetted arches and graceful stones of Egglestone Abbey, a Premonstratensian abbey of the late-1100s, founded by Ralph de Multon.

Abbey Bridge, 60ft/18.3m high, with a span of 75ft/22.9m, was built in 1773 as a toll bridge.

Immediately over the bridge, turn left with the Teesdale Way, on a prepared path east, known as Paradise Walk, alongside the Tees as it surges through its rocky gorge. At Mortham Lane, swing left, below Rokeby Park, descending to the confluence of the Tees and its tributary Greta, at the "Meeting of the Waters". Rise right, and cross Dairy Bridge high above a narrow gorge through which the Greta surges, a spot that inspired James Turner to produce a water-colour of Dairy Bridge.

Rise with the track to Mortham Tower, a defensive tower of the 1400s. Keep left, making for the waymarked gate to turn right. Stay with the cart track and leave the trees, left, to follow the waymarked route east and south by gate and stile, descending to the A66. Here a wide cemented underpass leads alongside the river to a stone stile at the east end of Greta Bridge, journey's end.

25 Doctor's Gate

This circular experience of forest and fell offers a profusion of interests, in particular for the botanist, ornithologist and industrial historian. Its many waymarked paths, fences and walls remove navigation problems, even in poor visibility.

Distance:
9½ miles/15.2km

Height gain:
853ft/260m

Walking time:
5 hours

Start/Finish:
Hamsterley Forest Visitor Centre. GR092313: 2 miles/ 3.2km west from Hamsterley, and 4½ miles/7.2km south of Wolsingham.

Type of walk:
A pleasing moderate walk along prepared forest paths, mine and quarry tracks, providing a variety of scenic delights.

Plentiful parking, at a nominal charge, adjacent to the visitor centre.

Hamsterley Forest Visitor Centre, with its many facilities, provides the perfect launch pad for this forest and fell journey. A few yards west from the visitor centre, beyond the staff car park, a stepped and waymarked way ascends right to a footbridge by a watertank; swing left and, at the first junction, left again.

A path flanked by a mix of silver birch, oak, beech and rowan, confirms that Hamsterley Forest, with its sixty different species, is not one of the dark monocultural cathedrals. It is a bird-blessed place, providing much pleasure to those who pass through. The arrow-straight track leads west-south-west for 800yds/m, passing two houses, to reach the Forest Drive by Low Redford Cottage. Opposite this creamy cottage, turn right at the pond on to a colour-coded waymarked prepared path that eases west alongside the tinkling waters of Ayhope Beck.

These man-made forest ponds support a variety of wild life: frogs, toads and newts, plus colourful meadow sweet, water avon, yellow flag and bullrush.

Continue west with the tree-lined beck for an attractive stroll through North Plantation and North Crag Wood to reach Metcalfes House.

Metcalfes House is a centuries-old coaching house or inn, previously known as "Honey Bee". Nestling in an idyllic setting, it provided rest and succour to those who travelled the Teesdale to Tynedale salt road. Its solid foundations, well-worn flags and steps no doubt housed animals as well as Metcalfe, who was, in all probability, the first landlord.

From Metcalfes House, with its picnic benches, walk south over Ayhope Beck for a short, sharp ascent on a sandy track to a waymarked five lane junction. Here a grass track leads west through the stately conifers to the forest boundary wall and, assisted by a stepped stile, passage is eased on to the heathery fell of Hamsterley Common. A faint grass path threads due west to two low marker cairns 150yds/m ahead, and

for the next 1¹/₄ miles/2km this sandy peat path, in places rutted, contours west-north-west above Ayhope Beck to the tree-ringed Shangri-La of Ayhope Shield at the Meeting of the Grains.

"Grain" is the Scandinavian or Norse epithet for "a branch of a stream", confirming the Norse influence in the North Pennines. Ayhope Shield is now a sad ruin, inhabited only by oak, sycamore and alder. The verdant confluence of South Grain Beck and North Grain Beck, ringed by the flat fells of Hamsterley Common and Pikeston Fell, provides entry to one of the most pleasing hidden valleys in the North Pennines.

Cross South Grain Beck to the ruin of Ayhope Shield, walking north-west with ageing thorn bushes and a broken dyke above the tree line, to leave the pastures over a plastic-bound fence stile descending with the trees to the stream below. It is on this descent that the pathway ahead can be seen spearing north-north-east through the heathery flanks above Steel Beck. Ford the stream by the ruined shieling and for the next 1¹/₄ miles/2km plod steadily on to the abandoned mineworkings on the ridge ahead (GR054337).

The pockmarks of man's efforts to wrest metals and minerals from the possessive grasp of the Pennine fells abound, many still sterile and barren from the effects of lead poisoning. However interesting these unsightly boils of waste appear to the uninitiated, DO NOT VENTURE TOO CLOSE TO DRIFT MINE, SHAFT, SINK HOLE OR QUARRY FACE – THEY ARE DANGEROUS!

A wide mine track slashes through the northern workings, ascending east-south-east by its left fork to a prominent, but poorly constructed, four-sided cairn on the ridge summit. Swing left through the heather to join an angled stone wall that serves as a guide for ³/₄ mile/1.2km, east and south-east past a few wind-blasted conifers to the gated green road at the Doctor's Gate on the district boundary.

Many green roads known locally as "carriers' ways" or "salt roads" bisect these moors, with Doctor's Gate marking the crossroads of the Teesdale to Tynedale salt road and the carriers' way of Stanhope Lane. Much-used over the centuries by cadgers and drovers, certain sections still bear the gouges trodden out by lines of laden packhorses; in others, well-worn road stones are visible.

From the walled gate, walk south with the salt road for 200yds/m, to turn left (east), on to the public path known as Stanhope Road/Lane, a way that eventually leaves the open fell, via quarry, cairn and conifer, to join the Wolsingham road at Hoppyland.

Swing right by White Lodge, descending to the hamlet of Bedburn. Prior to Bedburn Beck a public path travels south-west by the beckside for 800yds/m to end the walk at the visitor centre at Hamsterley Forest.

26 Slate Ledge to Frosterley

With ever-changing sights and sounds, the route travels the green and fertile fringes of Teesdale and the pleasing glades of Hamsterley Forest to the quarried floor of Weardale. Frequently threading its way via an old salt road, much-favoured by cadgers, drovers and miners, it provides the adventurous with an invigorating trek.

Distance:
15 miles/24km

Height gain:
1,129ft/344m

Walking time:
7 1/2 hours

Start:
Teesdale. GR993251:
1 mile/1.6km north-west from Eggleston.

Finish:
Frosterley. GR029370:
on the A689, 3 miles/4.8km south-east of Stanhope, and the same distance west from Wolsingham.

Type of walk:
A linear walk of character that provides many rewards. Over high fell paths, in places ill-defined, by forest tracks and waymarked paths, this journey can surprise even the most experienced.

Potentially confusing in poor visibility.

The signposted public bridleway on the north side of the B6278 provides the starting gate for this fine walk. Walk north with the cart track, taking the stony right leg past the disued quarry with Blackton Beck below right.

A waymarked gate opens up the heathery fell as the stony way winds north-west, where the only sounds are the curlew's cry and the bleating of a new generation of Swaledales. Beyond a rush-infested reservoir the track ascends north-east to the skyline rim of Slate Ledge.

Teesdale and Weardale slate is the dale's traditional roofing material. Although referred to as slate, it is in fact locally-mined sandstone. Known as Flagstone, a sandstone impregnated with mica chips, this rock can be split into thin workable sheets, or flags. Perhaps not so lasting as pure slate, this "dales slate", being local, is cheaper.

As Slate Ledge is breasted and the cart track heads east to Spurlswood Gill Head, a waymark leads left through tousy heather, heading north-east to the now visible conifers of Hamsterley Forest. Beyond the meltwater gully of Quarter Burn take the posted right fork for the final 3/4 mile/1.2km to the forest gate and shieling by Smithy Hirst Sike.

Hamsterley Forest, first planted in 1927, covers approximately 2,000 hectares and contains a visually pleasing mix of conifers and broadleaves, including spruce, larch, Scots pine, Douglas fir, beech, oak and birch. Inhabitants include roe deer, badger, red squirrel, fox and bats, plus many birds of prey, nightjar, woodpeckers, woodcock, etc..

The following wooded 5 1/2 miles/8.8km, with its maze of tracks, may produce dull repetitive instructions; fortunately not so the walk, particularly when exploring Pennington Beeches and Metcalfes House. At the forest perimeter track bear right (north-east), for a short distance to the first junction. Here a waymarked grass track turns right, later to swing left and proceed east then north-east to a T-junction bordering Pennington Plantation. At the junction turn right for a few strides before leaving the road, via a post on the left, to enter this small and unexpected beech wood.

Wander at will under these fine trees, but exit to the east, then walk left on the track for a few steps to run right and descend south-east for 800yds/m to a crossroads on the forest edge above Spurlswood Beck. For the next 2½miles/4km, the route progresses north-north-east along the Silver Mile, contouring above and parallel to Spurlswood Beck.

By the fork (take the left) at GR051275, look for the rowan sapling growing out of the rotting branch of a living roadside cherry.

The Silver Mile ensures height and direction are maintained until a major haul road is met, beyond Oak Bank and above Strawberry Bank. At this major forest road swing right, descending to crossroads above The Grove. This imposing house was once owned by the Surtees family, as was the estate that is now Hamsterley Forest. A few yards north of the crossroads descend left on a waymarked path to cross Euden Beck before ascending through the stately conifers on to a forest road travelling north to the junction at Potato Hill. Here a sandy track descends right to a new footbridge spanning Ayhope Beck and beyond to Metcalfes House, a centuries-old, partially-restored, inn, also known as "Honey Bee".

Continue north on a rising track, to leave the confines of the forest for the scarred skyline of the open fell of Cabin Hill. A treeside track rises left, before swinging north to wriggle through a scatter of disused quarries and rusting paraphernalia leading to the gated stone wall at Doctor's Gate. At the gate double back left, alongside the wall, on a broad grass track to a bisecting public path.

Known as Stanhope Road or Stanhope Lane, this was once a well-used mine and quarry road running to Stanhope in Weardale.

Turn right (west-north-west), on to a settled course over continuous moorland leading to a prominent cairn on the skyline ahead. When reached, this four-sided cairn, (1230ft/375m) provides extensive views over Pikeston Fell and Hamsterley Common.

Continue with the somewhat clearer twin track, to pass the craters and spoil that mark the disused mine, beyond which the now broad track swings right (north). At this point leave the track for a north-west course, via the faintest of heather fell paths, with only a minute cairn and the Elephant Trees as guides.

An elusive path with occasional small cairns assists passage for the 1 mile/1.6km to an access sign for walkers, prior to the wall and track of the Weardale Way east of the Elephant Trees. At the twin gates by the Weardale Way turn left and, with due reverence, pass the trees before reaching a waymarked gateway on the right. Here the descending stony way winds past Allotment House to the pretty, quarrying hamlet of White Kirkley before crossing the River Wear into Frosterley.

Frosterley, a settlement since the 1100s, rose to fame through Frosterley Marble, a hard, resilient, fossil-impregnated limestone which produces a distinctive product, similar to Purbeck Marble, and much favoured by church architects and monumental masons.

27 Coldberry and Hudes Hope

At every corner ever-changing views are revealed. Not all are aesthetically pleasing, but they combine to produce a walk of great interest. A journey that contains no severe inclines, although poor visibility may cause minor navigational problems on Hardberry Hill. Walk this miners' way, to what was the largest mine in Teesdale.

Distance:
8½ miles/13.6km

Height gain:
935ft/285m

Walking time:
4-4½ hours

Start/Finish:
Middleton-in-Teesdale. GR948254: on the north bank of the Tees at the junction of the B6277, B6282 and B6276; 10½ miles/ 16.8km north-west of Barnard Castle.

Type of walk:
An invigorating, rewarding circuit through dale-head desolation and beckside beauty. The journey covers country lanes, stony cart tracks, faint fellways, pasture tracks and permissive pathways.

Free car park in the market place.

Middleton-in-Teesdale is the unofficial capital and walking centre of Teesdale, whose central ornamental drinking fountain provides a traditional start for this and many other Middleton walks.

Middleton, a "Company Town" and northern administrative centre for the London Lead Company, known affectionately as the Quaker Company, rose from a 12th-century agricultural village. Indeed, names such as Seed Hill, Horsemarket and Market Place still remain. It was, however, in the 1800s that the town expanded in step with local lead production. The Quaker Company built not only up-to-date housing, but also many work places for the developing business and staff, and by 1842, the Teesdale Workman's Corn Association had established England's first 'Co-op'.

The cast-iron fountain, of 1877, was dedicated to company superintendent Robert Bainbridge. In 1905, the Quaker Company withdrew from Middleton.

Walk north from the fountain along Market Place, swinging left beyond the Teesdale Hotel to cross Hudeshope Beck and ascend west with Middle Lane, a lane that continues its steady ascent north-west for 2¼ miles/3.6km, by Middle Side and Bell House to Miry Lane junction. At the walled junction ahead (marked "No Through Road"), a public footpath marker indicates a right turn through the gate on to an ascending stony cart track. An alternative route, described later, via the prominent hush known as Coldberry Gutter, is available.

With the north-east guiding wall on the right, the track passes several small spoil heaps and two gates, to veer left through the pasture. Leave it as it swings left, and continue north-east with the wall. At the stone stile, switch sides and follow the wall to a stiled junction,

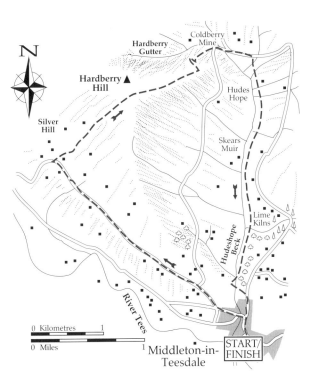

leading to out-bye pastures flanking the summit and triangulation point of Hardberry Hill. The east-north-east traverse is via a faint trod to a fence/wall junction. Here a narrow rail allows wallside passage east to a gate at its far end. (The OS map shows the right of way as passing through the wall, prior to the gate.)

The alternative route to this point involves an extra ³/₄ mile/1.2km via tracks and paths not marked as public paths. It does, however, allow considerate and careful walkers the opportunity to explore Coldberry Gutter by well-used miners' tracks. From the "No Through Road" sign continue north by lane and mine track, swinging right at each of the four forks, rounding Silver Hill to the huge gully of Coldberry Gutter.

"Hushing" was a technique used from the 1600s to the mid-1800s to strip the surface soil and rocks from the lead veins – in Coldberry's case 2½ million tons were removed by regular scouring. Torrents from overhead reservoirs, such as the nearby one on Coldberry Moss, cascaded down the fells sweeping away loosened debris, and creating the silent gullies and gutters we see today. The exposed galena was then gathered by hand; a keen eye may still spot a sample.

Ascend east with Coldberry Gutter, by mine track and path, leaving it by Hardberry Hill to pass through a metal gate and, with the adjoining wall on the right, descend east to the gate on the main route.With the surrounding mining memorabilia, descend north-east with the twin track to Hudes Hope, overlooked, and in places overshadowed, by the sheds, shafts and spoil of what was Coldberry Mine.

Coldberry Mine, the largest and the last lead mine to operate in Teesdale, closed in 1951; it leaves only the cries of the moorland birds and the sighing of the winds to ruffle today's silence.

Zigzag ways criss-cross the spoil to join a road that bridges Hudeshope Beck and ascends east below Lodge Sike Farm. Here a waymarked gate (yellow arrowhead) indicates a wallside path through an ill-drained pasture to the south. At the waymarked stile, turn left over the rocky bed of Marl Beck, passing two gated walls, to reach an arched drift mine entrance and accompanying mine shop below Marlbeck Gutter.

Mines cutting into the fellside are known in the North Pennines as "drifts" or "levels". The entrance, or portal, was arched with stone – cheaper and longer lasting than timbering – high and wide enough for the mine ponies to pass through. The tubs, pulled by the drift ponies, were of a standard design throughout the North Pennines – high and slender and emptied by a base trap door.

The southern aspect of Hudes Hope is today a pleasing sight, in spite of man's despoilation, for nature has restored much by carpeting the combed fellsides with grasses and larch. Stroll south by the beck, then by waymarked gated and stiled walled pastures the way passes Old Skears before entering the woods of Hudeshope Gill by a waymarked stile. From here a narrow stepped path winds down through a mix of timber to pass Skears Quarry and the preserved remains of several large limekilns.

With care descend to the roadway below, swinging left with the winding way for a relaxing 800yds/m, with the beck at its most winsome and colourful; in season sample the wild raspberries. At the right fork cross the beck, via a private vehicular bridge and permissive path, and for a short distance walk the true right bank of the narrowing gill to a footbridge leading left to the eastern bank. A dirt footpath now ascends through the trees, somewhat reluctantly, to meet the Stanhope road at Town Head. Turn right on this rapidly descending road past St. Mary's Church and Market Place to journey's end.

28 High Force and Gibson's Cave

Some walkers take a day to complete this circuit, along the floral banks of the Tees. It is a unique experience that cannot be surpassed within Britain's shores, and offers to all who tread its waymarked paths, magnificent waterfalls, including High Force, England's greatest, and the largest juniper "forest" in the United Kingdom.

Distance:
5¼ miles/8.4km

Height gain:
361ft/110m

Walking time:
2 hours

Start/Finish:
Bowlees Visitor Centre. GR907282: on the B6277, 4 miles/6.4km north-west from Middleton-in-Teesdale. Free car park/picnic area. Parking also at a roadside lay-by (GR906281), by Bowlees Farm.

Type of walk:
An impressive, although short, circular walk by waymarked paths (a riverside section of the Pennine Way), two footbridges, a short stretch of the B6277, a quiet country lane, and finally a gentle descent by farm track: constant excitement, and no navigation problems.

Bowlees Visitor Centre, easily reached from the signposted car park and picnic area, provides the perfect start for a perfect walk. The Centre, opened in 1976, is housed in a converted Methodist chapel of 1845 and provides a wealth of information about Teesdale for lovers of the great outdoors. Time spent here is time well spent.

Walk south from the centre, with the walled lane, to cross the B6277, passing through a kissing gate on to a field path leading to a stone stile slit, and stately conifers.

The Tees is now revealed, a breathtaking introduction to the river by Low Force and Wynch Bridge. Low Force, an intriguing two-step tumble between islands of dolerite, is also known as Salmon Leap.

The word "force", for waterfall, is Icelandic Norse in origin, as are "gill" and "beck", for valley and stream. Indeed, the extent of Scandinavian settlement in the northern Pennines can be traced by such nomenclature.

Wynch Bridge is a chain suspension footbridge, circa 1830, locally referred to as "Two Inch Bridge". It replaced the original miners' bridge of 1704, a structure that tragically collapsed during 1820, with haymakers on board, causing the loss of one life.

Once the bridge is crossed, turn right, and with the well-trodden turf of the Pennine Way and the musical waters of the Tees, wander north-west and west by the river's true right bank.

The banks and adjacent walled pastures attract botanists from the four corners of the globe to observe and study such arctic and alpine rarities (i.e. rare to Britain), as spring gentian, bog sandwort and alpine forget-me-not, in addition to orchids, ox-eye daisies and kingcups.

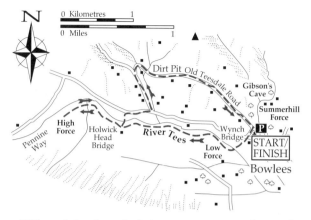

With such jewels underfoot, a common sense plea to all walkers: please keep to the designated paths.

At Holwick Head Bridge, continue with the Pennine Way, rising on a slabbed path to the gate and mapped notice board marking the perimeter of Upper Teesdale National Nature Reserve, England's largest. It also marks the entrance to a rare expanse of juniper, their twisted and tortuous branches blanketing the southern slopes above Keedholm Scar, and scenting the air with a distinctive aroma.

By now a beckoning rumble of thundering water will have filled the air and excited the senses, as the mighty cataract of High Force is approached. This eager advance must be tempered with caution and self-preservation, by sticking to the path and not straying too close to the sheer cliffs of the Whin Sill that rise high above the Tees.

High Force, one of northern England's major tourist attractions, spills its peat-stained brown waters over a dolerite and shale sill of 70ft/21m to pound out a bowl in the spray-filled theatre below. Not the highest of falls, but without doubt the greatest, its constant flow regulated in measured amounts from Cow Green Reservoir, high in upper Teesdale.

Return on the outward path through the juniper to Holwick Head Bridge, a way that provides reverse views of this most pleasing dale. Cross the gated bridge, over its wooden sleepers, to swing right and ascend with the tree-lined track to the B6277. Turn right for a short sharp dash east, before bolting left up the signposted Ettersgill road. This pleasant lane is soon abandoned by taking the right fork and descending to the tidy white-washed walls of Dirt Pit on the old Teesdale road.

Dirt Pitt, an uninviting name meaning "deerpeth" or deer path, stands on the site of a chapel for the foresters of Teesdale Forest, an area administered by Rievaulx Abbey. The old Teesdale road, closed 1820, ran through the Forest of Teesdale to Middleton-in-Teesdale.

This old way, now initially Tarmaced and gated beyond the white walls of Ash Hill, is followed east, descending to Bowlees, a track that provides ever opening views of Teesdale, in particular of Holwick Scars to the south and the deep-riven hushes of Coldberry Gutter on Hardberry Hill to the east. From the visitor centre return, via Bow Lee Beck, to the car park. Swing left on to the posted and waymarked Gibson's Nature Trail, leading north alongside the beck for 500yds/m to Summerhill Force, the third and final waterfall of the walk, a pencil-thin (compared with the previous two) 20ft/6m cascade shooting over the limestone entrance to Gibson's Cave, the hideout of a local reiver of the 1500s. Return on the outward path to Bowlees Car Park.

29 Cronkley Fell

Generations of Pennine Wayfarers have no doubt cast a discerning eye over Cronkley Fell, noting it down as a walk for the future. Perhaps, though, the most eager to tread these scenic miles are the ologists – entomologist, geologist, glaciologist, hydrologist, meteorologist, mineralogist, ornithologist, phytologist, potamologist and zoologist. Along this three-seasons walk, that might well be called "The Ologists' Trail", there are interests for all.

Distance:
9¼ miles/14.8km

Height gain:
705ft/215m

Walking time:
5 hours

Start/Finish:
Langdon Beck, a scattered hamlet on the B6277, 15 miles/24km south-east from Alston, and 8 miles/12.8km north-west of Middleton-in-Teesdale.

Type of walk:
A waymarked journey, over a unique fell and along the south bank of the Tees. A way that demands care in the placement of feet, over Pennine Way paths and farm lanes, grassy fell tracks, riverside trods with scattered rocks and wooden walkways.

Start from either Langdon Beck Hotel (GR853312), or Langdon Beck Youth Hostel (GR860305). Langdon Beck, and tempting sightings of Cronkley Fell and its rocky scars, hastens the desire to be up and walking.

From either hotel or hostel descend to Saur Hill Bridge, where the Pennine Way crosses the rock-strewn bed of Langdon Beck, a beck that signals the strength of its winter spates by the size and frequency of the boulders in its bed. Cross the stone stile at the north-eastern end of the bridge and, with the Pennine Way path, by wall and beck, walk south-east to meet the hurrying Tees, and beyond, the stressed structure of Cronkley Bridge.

This stretch typifies upper Teesdale, colourfully-carpeted with wild flowers such as violets, Canterbury bells and an unusual, pink-flowered yarrow. Ahead the flanks of High Knott and High Crags display rocky scars and accompanying boulder fields, with the Tees being simply itself.

Once over this limping bridge, with one pillar severely scarred, continue south with a winding farm road, ascending to Cronkley Farm, a building of naked stone that is somewhat of a rarity in Teesdale, as the majority of farmhouses are white, with black barns. At the steading descend as directed, on a signposted footpath to a stile bearing the acorn sign, and climb the stony path bisecting High and Low Crags. By stile and wall the Pennine Way rises to Bracken Rigg, bearing little bracken, but topped with a waymarked pole. Here the route leaves the Pennine Way, descending south to a crossroads and an information board marking the entrance to Upper Teesdale National Nature Reserve.

Although the open heathery fell is sacrosanct, walkers are catered for by the extensive waymarked track that winds

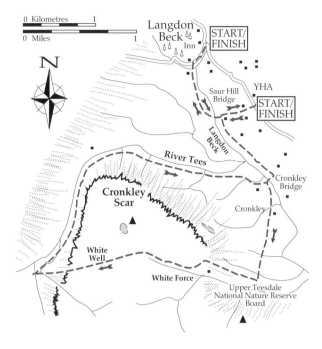

for 2 miles/3.2km across the upper reaches of Cronkley Fell. From this track the many interesting features of the fell can be observed, without having to flounder willy-nilly over prime grouse moor, on which grouse, curlew, plover, snipe and dunlin live a balanced life alongside the indigenous raptors.

Turn right at the grassy crossroads, ascending Birk Rigg via a wide grassy track to the rock-strewn summit of Cronkley Fell.

As ascent continues, the dry rock face of White Force is exposed beneath the summit rim. Listed as a waterfall, it *appeared in the hot dry summer of 1995 as a clone of the dry fall at Malham Cove. "Basaltic scaurs" at White Force are intersected by the Great Burtreeford Dyke, running in from Cowshill, Weardale; rocks said to contain little or no lead veins, yet spoil heaps, in all probability quarry waste, can be seen at White Force foot.*

On reaching the summit plateau, the now cairned way winds west passing three enclosed areas in the vicinity of White Well and White Well Green. The well seeping from the limestone is a popular meeting place for nomadic Swaledales and as such may prove to be undrinkable, even for the most drouthy of walkers.

The fenced enclosures surround areas of Sugar Limestone soil and its unique vegetation, plants that are much desired by the local Swaledale sheep and rabbit population, hence the enclosures, which hopefully will preserve the many unusual species.

Increasing numbers of trackside cairns assist passage as the narrowing path, overlooked by frequent indications of the MOD's presence above Black Sike, descends west beyond Man Gate to join the Tees at a small island east of Falcon Clints. Turn sharp right (north-east), for a real riverside walk of 2½ miles/4km. With the heavy traffic travelling along the opposite bank of the Tees by Widdy Bank Farm, a quiet journey can be enjoyed through heathery boulder-strewn trods and over some non-too-steady wooden walkways. Overlooked by the Whin Sill scars and boulder fields of Fox Earths, Raven Scar, Cronkley Scar, Green Hill Scar and Skue Trods, the path finally arrives at Cronkley Pastures and High House just prior to Cronkley Bridge. Cross the Tees by Cronkley Bridge to turn left and return to Langdon Beck.

30 High Hurth Caves

This circular waymarked walk is not only a gentle half-day hike of interest, but also a taster of the secret delights of upper Teesdale that lie hidden to the west. The walk is mainly on grass paths and hard-core tracks.

Distance:
4 miles/6.4km

Height gain:
426ft/130m

Walking time:
2-2½ hours

Start/Finish:
Langdon Beck Hotel.
GR853312: on the
B6277, 8 miles/12.8km
north-west of
Middleton-in-Teesdale,
and 5½ miles/8.8km
south from St. John's
Chapel.

Type of walk:
A circular stroll with an easy ascent to High Hurth Edge, over out-bye pasture paths, old quarry roads, farm tracks, burnside paths and a quiet lane.

Limited parking, with permission.

Langdon Beck, a scattered collection of whitewashed farms and cottages, offers several possible starts for this walk; convenience favours Langdon Beck Hotel or the youth hostel. Cross the road at the hotel to the

outbuildings and walk north-east and east on the
Tarmac lane and farm track, alongside the tumbling
waters of Langdon Beck, to the farm of Valence
Lodge. Pass through the gated yard and, by the quaint
house, cross the bridge over the beck to the pasture
beyond. Ahead the limestone escarpment of High
Hurth Edge, an immediate goal, can be seen on the
rim of High Hurth. Swing left through the gated wall,
and then right to traverse the grassy flanks east-south-
east on a trod that keeps below two three-walled
sheep shelters. The angled walls of these starred
shelters, known as "bields", provide shelter from
the harsh winds, no matter from which direction.

Continue the steady ascent, by pasture path, through
two gated walls and, before the third is reached, swing
left and rise to a gate immediately below the caved
limestone escarpment. Six narrow fissures snake into
the limestone, revealing little but the broken stumps
of stalactites. DO NOT ATTEMPT TO SQUEEZE
INTO THESE CAVES: ACCESS IS FOR POTHOLERS
ONLY.

An easy scramble to the summit of the Edge can
be made via the eastern end of cliffs alongside the
trickling sike.

*It is documented that in 1887, James Blackhouse, an
archaeologist, extracted from these caves a collection of
human and animal bones, later identified as belonging to
prehistoric man and over twenty animals, including lynx
and wolf. They are known locally as "Mawkin's Caves".*

Descend the rocks, by a sike that eventually disappears underground, then swing left on to the grass
pathway leading east to a track crossroads. Here the
route turns right (south), on a grassed-over cobbled
quarry road, passing through four gated walls to reach

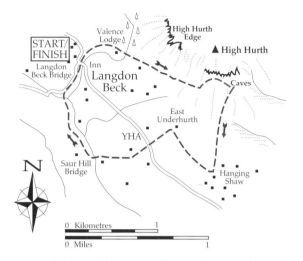

the buildings of Hanging Shaw. Hanging Shaw is home to several over-enthusiastic dogs; fortunately the dog-run is avoided by turning sharp right through yet another gate past an abandoned farmhouse, to walk north-west through colourful pastures to Hodge Hall and East Underthank. This is a tidy farm, one of many in upper Teesdale; its wide drive swings left to cross the B6277 close by the youth hostel, and descend by the white walls of New House to the Pennine Way at Saur Hill Bridge. Cross the bridge and immediately turn right at a gate to join the path running north with Langdon Beck. Continue along the true right bank, taking care to avoid the landslips, to emerge by stile almost into the backyard of Intake Farm at the confluence of Langdon Beck and Harwood Beck. The final water crossing, over what could be classified as a high ford or a low bridge, to the lane leads right (north), to Langdon Beck Hotel.

31 Cauldron Snout and Herdship

Four inspirational forms of North Pennine water accompany the walker over the high fells of upper Teesdale: a wild, far-seeing way, rich in unique upland wildlife and vegetation, that will impress and inspire.

Distance:
15 miles/24km

Height gain:
689ft/210m

Walking time:
7 1/2 hours

Start/Finish:
Langdon Beck. GR853311: on the B6277, 7 1/2 miles/12km north-west of Middleton-in-Teesdale.

Type of walk:
A long, but never demanding, circular journey of wonderment along prepared paths, Tarmac lanes, miners' ways, grassy tramways and cart tracks, with a little boulder hopping and rock scrambling for added interest.

Limited roadside parking.

Langdon Beck, more a state of mind than a village, provides an eminently convenient start from the hotel or the youth hostel. Waymarks direct the walker to the Pennine Way and Upper Teesdale Nature Reserve. This upland reserve, rising to 2,500ft/762m, is known world-wide as "The Teesdale Assemblage", where the altitude and rare Sugar Limestone rock combine to support an alpine mixture of flowers. Once on this hallowed route, follow it west by stile, gate and pasture path to join the River Tees, below the crags and boulder scree of Cronkley Scar. Beyond the white walls of Widdy Bank Farm, the narrowing valley swings south and west to Falcon Clints.

Pencil lead/shale was once produced at Widdy Bank Pencil Mill from a shale outcrop on Cronkley Scar. Falcon Clints, blocks of whinstone that colonnade skywards, were once home to golden eagles. Today, peregrine falcons sweep over the few twisted trees that cling to the towering cliffs.

Progress is now erratic, hopping over a shower of boulders and dashing over wooden duckboards. Stimulating and inspiring though this section is, it does little to prepare one for the sudden assault on the senses by the sights and sounds of Cauldron Snout above the confluence of the River Tees and Maize Beck.

Cauldron Snout is a booming, foaming cataract in which the peat-stained Tees is hurled 200ft/60m over a series of eight steps through a narrow gorge of Whin Sill. In the eyes and memories of many, this is the most spectacular waterfall in England. Today, even under the flow control of the reservoir valves, it is an awesome sight.

AVOID THE SLIPPERY ROCKS AT THE WATER-FALL'S EDGE. Several fatalities have occurred here, in-cluding the love-lorn "Singing Lady", who threw herself into the raging torrent, and whose ghost is said to haunt the rocky surrounds.

For those not wishing to scramble up the stepped rocks, a higher path rises on the fell to the right. By the Tarmac road beneath the dam, at the "PW" sign-post, turn right on to the nature trail path, in reality a Tarmac road for most of its 2 miles/3.2km. Ascend to

the east end of the 1,875ft/572m dam, from where the considerable expanse of Cow Green Reservoir sits comfortably in a circlet of high Pennine moors. Its north-western shore is highlighted by Meldon Hill and the undulating skyline of Great Dun Fell, Little Dun Fell and Cross Fell.

Cow Green Reservoir (770 acres/350 hectares, under 2,900 million gallons of water for Teesside) was constructed from 1967 to 1971 amidst a storm of controversy over the growing demand for water from industrial Teesside versus the preservation of this unique wilderness and its flora and fauna. One particular concern was that the vast area of water would warm in the summer sun and later raise the winter temperature. Cow Green Meteorological Station has recorded no significant change.

Continue north with the nature trail, by Sugar Lime-stone and weather station, where on the surrounding fells mountain pansy, thyme, bird's-eye primrose, harebell and the unique Teesdale violet, thrift and spring gentian grow. At a kissing gate turn left to Cow Green Car Park (GR811309).

Cow Green and upper Teesdale are riddled with the drifts and shafts of lead and mineral workings, where lead, crystalline barytes and purple fluorspar crystals were mined. Many can still be identified, others lie drowned beneath Cow Green Reservoir.

Above, spoil heaps pepper the flanks of Touting Hill, christened Lazy Hill as its banks were often used by resting miners. This area was also favoured as an overnight stop by drovers and their black highland cattle, hence its name.

The route can be split at this point by returning east, via the reservoir road over Cow Rake to Langdon Beck. Alternatively, walk from Langdon Beck, via the reservoir road to Cow Green Car Park.

From the car park walk north and north-west, by a waymarked gate, where a notice asks the walking public to "Take care and keep to the paths, particularly during nesting and lambing".

Here begins a classic section, of 4 miles/6.4km, with a height gain of 262ft/80m, that reveals much as it bounds over Herdship Fell above the leaden waters of Cow Green. After 1 mile/1.6km, the disused paraphernalia of Dubbysike Mine is met. Note the old mine shop renovated for shooters, with one room always open as a refuge for benighted travellers. Further up the trail lie more relics of Teesdale's mining past, this time Green Hurth Mine, parts of which have been transformed into sheep pens and shelters.

With the cleverly contouring tramway over Holdenhurth Band as a guide north, and the constant cries of the moorland birds as companions, the final 2 miles/3.2km to the B6277 and the ski-tows at Yad Moss below Burnhope Seat, are all too soon completed. Turn right (east), for a short distance on the verge of this Alston to Middleton road, then right again at the fork, where the original road sweeps over Spitley Tongue into the forgotten valley of Harwood.

Harwood Beck cuts a pastoral path into ever-widening Teesdale and then coaxes the eye to the distant Cleveland Hills and the North York Moors.

Descend south-east on the dirt and grass track into this green and pleasant valley, where the miner's hand can still be seen on the Cornish water pump at Lady Rake Mine. By gated Tarmac, the route passes flower-filled pastures and tidy white steadings, named Frog Hall, Herdship and Watersmeeting.

On the right by the beckside, note the church and school of St. Jude's, both once again sad and sightless ruins. Continue with the road, and prior to Force Foot, swing right on a public path leading to the north bank of Harwood Beck and Low End Bridge. Here the lane is rejoined, and the beck crossed, for the final $2^1/_2$ miles/ 4km, via Marshes Gill, Honey Pot Cottage and Peghorn Lodge to join the reservoir road swinging left to Langdon Beck and journey's end.

BALDERSDALE AND LUNEDALE

East of the Durham/Cumbria boundary, over the rolling wastes of Stainmore Common and Lune Forest, there are two dales that feed the Tees between Barnard Castle and Middleton-in-Teesdale – Baldersdale and Lunedale. They are dales, initially fashioned in the Ice Age, then polished by wind and water for thousands of years, that were restructured by the hand of farmer, forester, quarryman and miner. Then, from the 1880s, came the dam builders, to construct the five reservoirs that fill today's dales.

In the upper reaches of Baldersdale, Balderhead is surrounded by heather, heath and grouse moor, and below its dam nestles placid Blackton, home to a nature reserve, and the halfway mark of the Pennine Way. Below Blackton is Hury, set in a patchwork of green pastures.

Lunedale now plays host to two reservoirs, Selset sits high in the upper valley, flanked by the rough grazing land of Mickleton Moor and Cocklake Side, whilst Grassholme below basks in a pastoral setting of flowering meadows, interlaced with drystone walls.

Northumbrian Water who administer the reservoirs are committed to providing recreational facilities. They also recognise that the variety of habitats on and around the reservoirs provide valuable havens for wildlife. With a balanced mix of outdoor activities, conservation and the declaration of nature reserves and Sites of Special Scientific Interest, they have helped to create and maintain an environment that pleases.

In addition to the Pennine Way that passes through both dales, paths and tracks for walkers are waymarked, with information boards and picnic places at strategic points. Only two walks are detailed here, but there are others available from the visitor centre at Grassholme Reservoir.

Baldersdale is only a short distance along country lanes from the B6277, either from Cotherstone or Romaldkirk. Lunedale is accessible from the B6276, or the B6277 from Mickleton.

Car parks are available at all reservoirs.

32 Blackton and Goldsborough

This circuit, alongside Hury, Blackton and Balderhead Reservoirs over Cotherstone Moor and Ladyfold Rigg to Goldsborough, provides a wealth of visual, historical and wildlife experiences. The route passes a nature reserve, a Site of Special Scientific Interest (SSSI), carved rocks and Birk Hat Farm, former home of Hannah Hauxwell.

Distance:
10 1/2 miles/16.8km

Height gain:
797ft/243m

Walking time:
5 1/2 hours

Start/Finish:
West Briscoe car park in Baldersdale, at the south end of Hury Reservoir dam. GR966192: 3 miles/ 4.8km west of Cotherstone, and 7 miles/11.2km north-west of Barnard Castle via the B6277 and a minor road.

Type of walk:
A circular journey of contrasts; pastoral by waterside paths, dams and walled lanes, before rising on to occasionally damp sections of open fell, including the Pennine Way, and culminating in the rock and grass cap of Goldsborough.

Hury Reservoir, built in 1894, glistening beneath a patchwork of flowering meadows and tree-lined gills, is the oldest and most easterly of Northumbrian Water's three Baldersdale reservoirs. Its car park, with informative panel and map, makes a logical outset. Walk right (west) from the signposted car park on a country lane alongside the by-wash channel (an overflow for the higher reservoirs), to the water authority's green metal gate leading to Little Hury.

As the lane progresses west, immediate skyline sightings of the millstone grit caps of Shacklesborough and Goldsborough, guardians of this Norseman's dale, heighten the interest and quicken the step. Likewise, Little Hury, a small subsidiary reservoir used for training by outdoor centres, draws the walker to cross the footbridge and grassy embankment to the north bank leading to Blackton Dam and Reservoir.

Blackton, the smallest of Baldersdale's reservoirs, was constructed in 1896 for the Stockton and Middlesbrough Water Board. Emptied in 1993 for maintenance, but now fully replenished, it has on its western wetlands a nature reserve much-favoured by breeding waders, birds immune to, but no doubt grateful for, the lengthy name of their reserve – Site of Particular Ecological Importance (SPEI).

Continue along a waymarked concrete and grassy track, between wall and water, by the picturesque north shore of Blackton. The concrete was thoughtfully laid to allow access for the vehicles of the not-so-nimble, as the shoreline leads to Birk Hat Farm, the Pennine Way and an SSSI.

Birk Hat, much publicised one-time home of dales farmer, Hannah Hauxwell, is now a private house. The SSSI is on Hannah's Meadows, pastures that were farmed by Hannah in the traditional way, i.e. never cut until July, when the many indigenous grasses and flowers had seeded, thus allowing all to flourish. A nearby converted barn acts as an interpretive centre.

From Birk Hat, swing north with the Pennine Way to Birk Hat Hills, where a public path leads west, by the tree-sheltered High Birk Hat Farm, to the picnic area at the north end of Balderhead Dam.

Balderhead, overlooked by the heather-skirted and cairned cap of nearby Shacklesborough, was built in 1965 to supply water to industrial Teesside. The youngest and the largest of Baldersdale's reservoirs, it cradles 4 million gallons held back by a massive dam, 3,030ft/924m long and 156ft/48m high. Its dam top walk unfolds contrasting views of pleated fells and timeless pastoral peace by Blackton, Hury and beyond.

> *"Then, Balder, one bleak garth was thine, And on sweet brooklet's silver line."*
>
> *(Rokeby, Walter Scott.)*

Once over the dam, the road, but not the spirit, descends left with winding lane to Blackton (Baldersdale) Youth Hostel and Blackton Bridge. This is half-way house for Pennine wayfarers; for the optimist, 135 miles/216km completed, for the pessimist, another 135 miles/216km to do!

Turn right (south), with the Pennine Way, on a hardy track ascending to Clove Lodge, beyond which a grassy pathway continues south over the high-veld of Cotherstone Moor and Peatbrig Hill for 1 mile/1.6km to Race Yate. A junction of boundary lines, an angled stone wall with crossing pathway, and a PW sign, mark the left turn on to the east-bound public path over Race Yate Rigg, to the military track at Ladyfold Rigg and Ladyfold Crags. Take care at the outset not

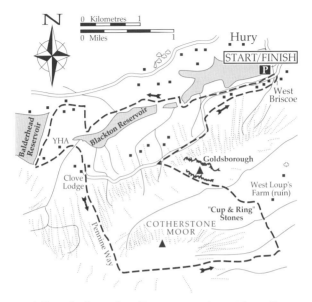

to follow the boundary line east-north-east from Race Yate.

The MOD boundary, an alien land advertised as "Army Training Area. Danger. Keep Out", signals a left turn on to the "PW Bowes Alternative", crossing Blackpool and Hare Sikes to reach what was once West Loups's Farm.

At this point keep your eyes down, not just to avoid the desolation to the east, but to spot some cup and ring marks. Close by two silver birch, not 10 yds/m from the PW as it passes West Loups's, these concentric rings surrounding deep cup marks can be found decorating two earthfast boulders. Such symbols, attributed to the Bronze Age, are thought to relate to life and death, as they also decorate tombs, cists and standing stones.

Continue north-west with the Pennine Way over the rush-ridden dampness of How Beck Head and Yawd Sike, to the rearing rock of Goldsborough, again a stride or so off the Pennine Way, and one of the day's highlights. From its grass-topped, wind- and rain-worn, millstone cap, views unfold of distant Teesdale and the high Pennines, confirming that much more awaits the adventurous.

Return to the Pennine Way, before forking right and dropping to the lane above Mere Beck Farm, turn right with the Tarmac – the verge is grassy and wide – swinging left by the gated grid to a waymark opposite Pitcher House. Abandon the Tarmac at this point for pastures green, via a public waymarked path (yellow arrowheads), leading east over stiles of stone to Scoon Bank and West Briscoe. From here it is but a short step to the road and the car park by Hury Dam.

33 Lunedale Round

A fine four-seasons walk through peaceful Lunedale, gilded by the shimmering ribbon of Grassholme; a timeless pastoral scene enhanced by an extensive and unique range of wildlife. Here is a dale mellowed and softened by its reservoirs. Allow time for photography, flower identification and birdwatching. The waymarked route is easy underfoot, allowing sturdy trainers in dry conditions.

Distance:
6 miles/9.6km

Height gain:
410ft/125m

Walking time:
3 hours

Start/Finish:
Grassholme Reservoir Visitor Centre. GR948225: 1 ¼ miles/ 2km west of Mickleton via a signposted minor road.

Type of walk:
A relaxing, figure-of-eight walk, encircling one reservoir and visiting another. There are two gentle ascents on quiet country lanes, with the majority of the miles over waterside paths.

Free car park, plus other amenities at the visitor centre.

Grassholme Reservoir Visitor Centre Car Park, at the eastern end south of the dam, provides the perfect start and finish for Lunedale walkers. Walk west, along the water's edge, from the visitor centre, to pass through a small gate.

The construction of Grassholme Reservoir began in 1910, but it was not until 1924 that work was completed. This included a link with the Baldersdale reservoir of Hury; ventilation pillars for the pipeline are visible on Bull Hill and by the western perimeter of Brownberry Plantation. The pipeline can be seen crossing the water between Grassholme Bridge and Selset Weir.

The entire walled south bank of Grassholme lies ahead, with the distinct grass/dirt pathway never far from the lapping water, a route, assisted over the inlets by wooden footbridges, that provides pleasing views of the serried ranks of buttercup meadows, and grey stone walls rising high above the north bank.

Continue beyond Brock Scar, where the five arches of Grassholme Bridge come into view, before walking over a raised ridge (glacial drumlin) to pass through a metal gate leading right by a narrow road to the bridge. Pause awhile, looking west over Selset Weir, a nature reserve, to the massive embankment that is Selset Dam.

Once over the bridge, rise with the lane for 1 mile/ 1.6km, passing Grassholme Farm and Low Selset, to reach the quarried flanks of Scarth Hills alongside the B6276 – Middleton to Brough road. At Lanehead Cottage, turn left and almost immediately left again, to cross the bill-boarded cattle grid leading down to Selset Dam. From the north end of Selset Dam descend south-east, passing two boulders, on an indistinct path parallel with Selset's slipway. Cross the waterside metal stile, with hooped handrail, and the bridge

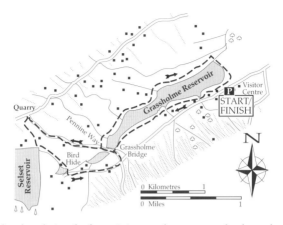

by the sluice, before rising to the waymarked road-side gate. Turn left for the bird hide entrance.

This small nature reserve, established in 1957, is home to approximately 900 breeding pairs of black-headed gull, plus widgeon, oystercatchers, snipe, lapwing, heron, grey wagtail, short-eared owl and swallow, whilst jackdaws nest in disused rabbit burrows.

From the hide continue east, ascending with the lane to How and the conifers of Brownberry, before descending to and crossing Grassholme Bridge. At the car park at its north end, turn right on to the waymarked grass path that follows the north shoreline of Grassholme east, a way that winds, with deep and steep tree-lined inlets, for 1¹/₂ miles/2.4km, presenting a panorama of the shimmering water reaching to the castellated valve tower and dam. Framed by the skyline are silhouettes of Ever Rigg and Coldthorn Nook, their domes separated by the saddle of Slate Ledge. Cross the dam, with its twin slipways snaking down to the wooded banks of the River Lune, for the return to the visitor centre.

EAST FELLSIDE

*"The meals and bread stuffs were chiefly brought
from the valley of the Eden over the rough mountain passes on the backs of ponies."*

*(19th-century report by William Wallace
of the London Lead Company.)*

*East Fellside is somewhat of an idiosyncratic misnomer,
being the great western bastion of the North Pennines,
and not the east fellside. No doubt it was given that name
on a county basis, being the east fellside of Cumberland,
and not the western wall of the northern Pennines.*

*Regardless of its title, this wall of rearing fells provides
an almost impenetrable obstacle along its entire length, to
those wishing to enter the North Pennines from the Vale
of Eden.*

*From Brough to Brampton, the Pennines stretch from the
dark shales of Roman Fell and the conical slate Pike of
Murton (now in the out-of-bounds Warcop Firing Range),
by the great Whin Sill ravine of High Cup Gill and the
Pikes of Dufton and Knock, the massif of Cross Fell and its
outliers, Dun Fell and High Cap. And so north, over the
clean limestone lines of Melmerby Fell, to the endless wastes
of England's watershed, by Croglin Fell to Cold Fell.*

*A barrier that does not enjoy good weather, often hidden
by sullen cloud and lashed by tempestuous and fractious
winds, its heights remain an unseen mystery to many. For
those on whom the East Fellside sun shines, there are
rewards beyond compare, for the views from Cross Fell, the
highest Pennine of all, and Melmerby Fell will, once seen,
never be forgotten. Such treks require careful planning and
an abundance of good fortune.*

There are many walks that typify East Fellside, although only four are detailed here. One is short and tranquil, the others are for experienced hill walkers. Know yourself and your hills, for the conditions can, and frequently do, change with surprising speed.

East Fellside can be seen and reached from the A66(T), the M6 and A69(T) by a network of twisting country lanes to the many villages that nestle at its feet. Only one road bisects its awesome west wall, and that is the A686, Penrith to Alston road over Hartside Pass, a tortuous zigzag, surveyed and reconstructed by that outstanding 19th-century roadmaster, John 'Tar' McAdam, in 1824.

34 Hilton and Langton

The charming fellside villages of Hilton and Murton lie overshadowed, but unspoiled, by Warcop Training Range, an MOD-restricted area that engulfs and contaminates many acres of East Fellside, including the western bastions of Roman Fell, Mell Fell and Murton Pike. Fortunately, there are no such constraints on this gentle countryside walk. Rich in flora and fauna, the walk reveals an insight into Cumbrian rural life.

Distance:
5 miles/8km

Height gain:
328ft/100m

Walking time:
2½-3 hours

Start/Finish:
Hilton. GR735207: 3½ miles/5.6km east of Appleby-in-Westmorland, and the A66(T), via an unclassified road.

Type of walk:
A relaxing, low-level circular Eden Vale walk, by pasture and grassy common paths, beckside trails, farm tracks and quiet country lanes. A pastoral walk with many interests.

Limited lay-by parking at the extreme east end of the village.

Hilton, a green village of water troughs, stone-lined pumps and a pub, creates the mood for this walk.

Walk west through the tidy village of Hilton, and at the T-junction turn right, descending with the lane towards Hilton Beck Bridge. Prior to the bridge a sign-post ("Public Footpath, Langton") indicates a left turn to a grass track running west with Hilton Beck.

Hilton is a village that took its name from the owner of the manor, Hilton Hall, which bears a date of 1682. Of greater significance are the village water pumps. Installed by the London Lead Company (the Quaker Company), they are thought to be the first piped water supply in England.

A pleasant beck-side path reveals much as it journeys west. Note the eroded curves in the beck, indicating seasonal flash-floods, as the way progresses to cross Deep Gill, on stepping stones.

A gentle bracken-clad rise leaves the beck side to pass the southern end of the broadleaves of Ashbank Wood, where a colourful carpet of bluebells bursts forth in late spring. Ahead lie the walled pastures of Stoneriggs Farm, which can be seen to the left, and beyond, a pond known as Brackenber Flodders pro-vides a hazard for the local golf course. Keep to the right at a trident of tracks, and make for the waymarked gap stile in the wall. Here a post ("Langton") signals a wall-side path south-west to the wall's corner.

The skyline to the west is silhouetted by the Lakeland peaks, to the south the hogsbacks of the Howgills lead the eye left to the distinctive whaleback escarpment of Wild Boar Fell, and the long dark line of Mallerstang Edge.

From the wall corner descend diagonally west on a

grassy public path, crossing several fairways of the golf course (beware flying golf balls!) to reach the house and barn of Ellerholme. Take the right pathway, and follow the beck downstream to a ford and footbridge by the weathered outcrops of scarred old red sandstone. Once over the footbridge at Langton, swing right with the track, through a gate and across a road, to Langton Field. The public path passes between the farmhouse and the steading, and continues north-west on cart tracks offering enticing views of the rising pikes of East Fellside, in particular Cross Fell, Dufton Pike and the maw of High Cup, to meet the road from Appleby to Low Barn Farm.

By Langtonfield lie faint traces of dwellings that were razed to the ground in 1388 by marauding reivers from the north. Whether Border Scots or Northumbrian, the raiders' origins remain unclear.

Turn right on to this quiet lane and follow it north-east to Low Barn Road end, continuing north-east with a wide stone track, descending between the trees to Murton Beck. Do not cross, but swing right as directed by the post, to Shepherd's Cottage, then rise east through the surrounding waymarked pastures. Continue east by a stiled way and, on descent, cross Murton Beck by a small footbridge and ascend to Murton via Town Foot Farm.

Murton can trace its roots to 1283, when Murton Hall was recorded as a manor house of the Musgrave family. A wander around the village reveals many dates and owners' names.

Leave Murton south, via the Hilton road, for 500yds/m, passing a former Methodist chapel, circa 1837, before reaching what was Thwaites School, founded in 1738.

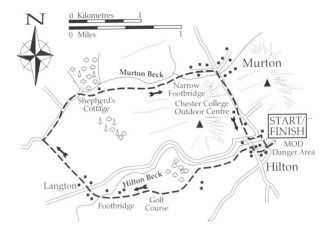

At the original school yard bear right, over a stile, for a pastoral passage back to Hilton, past St. John's Church.

Weddings and funerals, prior to 1863, were conducted in Appleby-in-Westmorland, after which it was the custom for newly-married couples to race back to the villages on horseback. A fatal riding accident resulted in the granting of parish status to Murton-cum-Hilton and the church of St. John.

As the road below Hilton Beck is reached, turn left to the houses ahead, and where the road bends left, leave it to cross a packhorse bridge and ascend the narrow pathway to the village green.

35 High Cup Nick

The well-trodden walk-in, though pleasant, does not prepare the hill walker for the explosion of unique and unexpected rocky scenery that awaits in, above and beyond the jaws of the Rundale ravine. Backstone Edge requires careful navigation, should visibility deteriorate, just as the vertiginous rim of High Cup requires common sense.

Distance:
11 1/2 miles/18.4km

Height gain:
1,670ft/509m

Walking time:
5 1/2-6 hours

Start/Finish:
Dufton. GR691250: 3 3/4 miles/6km north from Appleby-in-Westmorland and the A66(T).

Type of walk:
A circular high-level walk on mine tracks and sections of the Pennine Way, in addition to unmarked sections of open fell and boulderfields.

A walk for a clear day, by experienced walkers.

Public car park and toilets are available east of the post office.

Dufton, a timeless fellside village, provides a scenic springboard. From the red sandstone fountain on the green, walk east, past stately beeches by Dufton Hall Farm (circa 1779), leaving north-east on a signposted lane ("Pennine Way and public bridleway to High Scald Fell").

The name Dufton, with the prefix "duf", a dove or dove-cote, and the suffix "ton", a farm, indicates Angle and Saxon influence. For centuries it remained an agricultural community.

Then came the lead klondyke to East Fellside in the 18th and 19th centuries, and with it the Quaker-run London Lead Company, the most philanthropic of lead masters. It was an event that changed the village to what we see to-day, including the fountain, donated around 1858, by a Mr Wallace of the LLC. It bears a Latin inscription from Ovid's Metamorphoses, Book III, the story of Narcissus, a handsome lad who fell in love with his own reflection.

The inscription can be read from the fountain, and for non-classical scholars, it translates "There is a clear pool, whose waters gleam like silver. It is not tainted by the shepherds, or by the she-goats grazing on the mountain. Nor is it muddied by cattle, or by birds or wild animals, or by a branch fallen from a tree."

Surrounding the rectangular village green are post office, youth hostel and welcoming inn in this friendliest of villages, which today is also a link in the Pennine Way chain.

Beyond the houses the signposted Pennine Way veers left and the route ascends north-east on a narrow cart track, by lonely Pusgill House, above Pus Gill. As it rounds the skirts of conical Dufton Pike, the great gash of Little Rundale Beck can be seen ahead, below Backstone Edge.

This beck, fed by Little Rundale Tarn on Dufton Fell, disgorges into the River Eden, running on to the Irish Sea. Its larger neighbour, Great Rundale Tarn, spills not into

Great Rundale Beck but into Maize Beck and the North Sea. The watershed of England lies between the two tarns.

Once Dufton Pike is encircled, past a glacial moraine, Brownber Hill can be seen ahead. The grass/stone track swings right (north-east), to enter the rock-strewn gully of Great Rundale. This serious and for-bidding rock-lined gorge, gateway to the dark places, is surprisingly easy to enter. Pass through and leave thanks to a contouring main mine/quarry track by Threlkeld Side, which, in spite of the ankle-bending stones on the steep sections, soon leads, with some aplomb, to a shooters' hut by Great Rundale Tarn in a heather-clad wilderness.

Great Rundale has yielded galena, barytes and quarried stone. Lead extraction ended with the 1800s, barytes (barium sulphate) was mined until 1923, after which some spoil heaps in upper Great Rundale were graded for dis-carded minerals.

From the peat and heather surrounds of Great Rundale Tarn, return to the head of Great Rundale, using the old south side mine track above the scat-tered spoil in the gully floor. Take the left fork, from the track of ascent, rising south for approximately 800yds/m on a narrowing crescent of a twin track, to reach a large untidy stone cairn and a stone and post cairn. Beyond stands a stone and cement trig pillar (2,270ft/692m), above the hushed cleavage of White Rake.

This is a place from which to gaze west, over the green patchwork of the Vale of Eden, to the saw-toothed skyline of Lakeland, and to ponder on the next stage of the walk, along the boulderfields of Backstone Edge. It is a way of thin trods, squeezing between scattered stones, that is not a designated public path, but is a

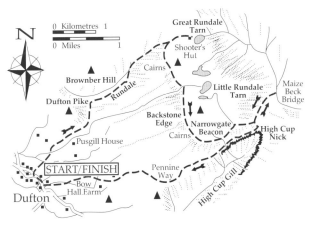

recognised route from Great Rundale to High Cup, and if adhered to should present no access problems.

In clear conditions, the journey south along the rim of Backstone Edge will present no problems, as it rounds the watery and rocky outfall of Little Rundale Tarn into Little Rundale Beck, 500yds/m from the trig pillar. Continue for a further ³/₄ mile/1.2km to skirt a dark and devious collection of peat hags, with a line of prominent stone cairns to the right. Beyond these swing left (east), on a grass path along the stony rim, to the large cairn-topped heap of stones known as Narrowgate Beacon, high above High Cup Gill. Should visibility be poor, tread a degree or two east of south, on the boulderfield's edge, with the outfall, the peat hags and the cairns as markers, to Narrowgate Beacon.

The Whin Sill escarpments, basalt stacks, precipitous grassy steps and lower slopes of boulders and scree that make up High Cup Gill, defy description. Viewed from Narrowgate

Beacon, this 1,000ft/305m ravine is the wonder of the North Pennines. The view far outstrips that enjoyed by Pennine Wayfarers who travel a lower path.

From the Beacon continue north-east for 600yds/m on a thin path with the limestone outcrops, before winding down the grass slopes of the declining rim. Join the stone-marked grass path of the Pennine Way leading north-north-east to Maize Beck footbridge, an easy and short moorland walk to the oft-surging waters of Maize Beck, fed by Great Rundale Tarn, and its delightful limestone mini-gorge.

Return to High Cup Nick and, with the well-trodden and cairn-marked Pennine Way, descend by the northern rim of High Cup Gill, passing Dod Hill and Bow Hall Farm, for the final 3½ miles/5.6km to Dufton.

The term "nick" refers to the point where a pencil-thin waterfall spears over the rocky edge, and in times of gale force winds actually spirals skywards.

Note also the prominent, and somewhat unstable, basaltic stack known as Nichol's Chair, or Last, some 500yds/m west from High Cup Nick. It was named after a cobbler from Dufton, who climbed the stack and is reputed to have cobbled a pair of boots on its summit.

Fox hunts, with a difference, take place in High Cup Gill, where huntsmen on foot scour the steep slopes with the hounds.

36 Kirkland and Cross Fell

Fiend's Fell, Cross Fell's original, perhaps more appropriate, name, is a fickle and ever-changing besom. Although ranked eleventh among the mountains of England, Cross Fell is unknown by many and unwalked by most, with the exception of the annual pilgrimage of Pennine Wayfarers. This walk can surprise and delight with its ever-changing and distant views, its surfeit of upland wildlife and its intriguing past. But be prepared for Cross Fell's mood swings.

Distance:
9½ miles/15.2km

Height gain:
2,297ft/700m

Walking time:
6 hours

Start/Finish:
Kirkland. GR648325:
6 miles/9.6km north
from Kirkby Thore, and
5½ miles/8.8km east of
Langwathby.

Type of walk:
Circular, upward and
onward for walkers who
enjoy a challenge. Never
exposed but always
demanding, the route
treads a variety of paths,
from stony cart tracks to
unmarked open fell.

Limited verge side
parking, but take care
not to obstruct residents'
access.

Kirkland, a small, friendly East Fellside village with few external facilities, provides a pleasant base for the ascent of Cross Fell. From Kirkland walk east, to signposted Ranbeck Farm, on a public Tarmac lane. Maps show a public bridleway from Kirkland Hall to Ranbeck, a way that is not clear on the ground and involves passing through several gates and sheep pens; for the convenience of both walker and farmer, take the lane to Ranbeck.

The Hanging Walls of Mark Anthony are a series of ill-defined ridges thought to be Roman cultivation terraces, south-west from Ranbeck. Did the nearby Roman Maiden Way prompt the Mark Anthony connection?

At Ranbeck, cross the beck and swing right (south), with a farm track to the field gates of Wythwaite House. Pass through three gates, turning left on to a walled strip of grass and gorse, rising east from Blencarn. Continue east through the scrub, with this funnelling green road, before breaking out on to the bracken-clad approaches to Grumply Hill. This grass-clad domed mound channels the eye and the feet, via a fine grass contouring path, to the outcrops crowning the heights of Wildboar Scar, the first of several high steps to Cross Fell.

The green road was used as a permanent funnelling corral by local farmers around Blencarn. Into it summered stock would be driven from the high fells to overwinter on in-bye pastures around the villages.

Animals were not alone in rushing down Cross Fell's western flanks, there is also The Helm (hilltop) Wind, a local easterly wind of great ferocity that roars along the fellside, capable, at its most fractious, of toppling a loaded mini-bus. The village of Milburn is the recipient of The Helm's most violent moments.

The seemingly impenetrable cliffs of the scar are approached by a steep, no-nonsense grass path, rising north to a cairned trod at Sturba Nook, which provides fine views west. Swing right (north-east), above Wildboar Scar with cairns and trod, to traverse the stony plateau ahead, for now the landscape has donned a harder, sterile mantle. Restructured in places by the lead miner's hand, there is little to assist passage to the Pennine Way and Tees Head save for a few marker cairns, fingers of stone, small stone piles and a clear day. For the next 1½ miles/2.4km northeast, with Cross Fell's summit cap and its circlet of boulders now clearly visible (hopefully), the steadily rising trod ascends just one more small scar, before reaching the Pennine Way.

The original name of Fiend's Fell was expunged by the building of a cross and altar on the summit (hence the name

Cross Fell), where a mass was held by a leading cleric of the day. Several have been credited, none confirmed, with this good deed of the early 1500s.

The crosspath is marked with an inset stone slab, inscribed north and south "PW", and east and west with the bridleway symbol, a horseshoe. Continue east for 300yds/m to Tees Head, the source of the River Tees, for on this watershed, around GR700340, there are any one of a dozen oozing seepages trickling from the bible-black peat, that could claim to be Tees Head.

Return to the inscribed slab and turn right (north-west), on to the Pennine Way. A short, sharp bouldery ascent up the final escarpment, past a tall marker cairn, leads over a flat grassy way to the trig pillar and walled shelter, at 2,930ft/893m, the high point of the Pennines.

The profusion of summit cairns, particularly those on the escarpment rim, tend to confuse walkers. Why are they all there? The simple answer is that the cairns on the summit extremity, built centuries ago, post a warning, in poor visibility, of the presence of steep boulderfields.

"Walk along the crest of Crossfell and so to Alston, and you will learn at once what follows on an untouched soil from the absence of a track/guide. One ravine out of many radiating from a summit will lead you to one valley you seek; take another and you are condemned to traverse mountains in order to repair the error. In fog or at night there is nothing to help you." (Hilaire Belloc, The Old Road.*)*

To leave the summit there is a choice. In clear weather, walk west to the summit rim, turn right, to follow the escarpment north and east, for 500yds/m of far-reaching views. At the cairned Pennine Way, turn left (north), to descend through a boulderfield to reach a large marker cairn, turning left at the old coffin or corpse road for Kirkland. In bad weather and poor visibility, strike north from the trig pillar, with the cairns on the PW, to the boulder slopes and the coffin road.

The coffin or corpse road was so called as it was used to convey the departed from Garrigill to Kirkland, there being no consecrated ground in Garrigill at that time. Indeed, it was only after a coffin was dumped on the fell during a snowstorm and left for two weeks before recovery, that ground in Garrigill was consecrated, or so the story goes.

The final 3^1/$_2$ miles/5.6km of descending cairned track, west and south-west to Kirkland, is what you make of it. It can be a delight, with an explosion of varying views, accompanied by the sights and sounds of the moorland birds as the way winds between the ravine of Ardale Beck and the summit escarpment of High Cap.

Continue to the gated pastoral acres of Kirkland Hall, now tastefully converted into holiday cottages, and the village of Kirkland.

37 Melmerby Fell

By its length and unremitting inclines, over unmarked fells that have a reputation for deteriorating weather, this is a journey for experienced hill walkers. It is an invigorating trek, with many rewards, for on a clear day it equals the traverse of Cross Fell. For solitude-seekers, the silence is broken only by the cries of the moorland birds and the sighing wind.

Distance:
12 1/2 miles/20km

Height gain:
1,936ft/590m

Walking time:
6-7 hours

Start/Finish:
Kirkland. GR648325:
5 1/2 miles/8.8km east of Langwathby, and 6 miles/9.6km north from Kirkby Thore by the A66(T).

Type of walk:
A challenging high-level hike, laid out in the form of a dumbbell, treading quiet country lanes, cart tracks, woodland paths, pasture paths, quarry inclines, open fell trods and boulderfields.

Limited parking on the verges. Do take care not to restrict access.

The quiet friendly hamlet of Kirkland, nestling below the omnipotent massif of Cross Fell, provides both atmosphere and an ideal start. From the little church of St. Lawrence walk west with the lane for 500yds/m to the gated entrance to Bank Hall (signposted "Public Bridleway Maiden Way"). Turn right (north) along a drive that offers enticing views of the rising sweeps of fellside. At the gateway leading to Bank Hall, turn left. Here a waymarked gate allows diagonal passage over a pasture to a solitary oak and an old barn, prior to a waymarked gate ahead. Carry on with the cart track, past two gates and making for a third, to enter the woods on the right, via a stone stile tucked into the wall corner by that third gate.

Once in this oak wood a faint grass path swings left, and with the waymark rises right, to the embankments of a prehistoric settlement.

The faint path continues north-east through the elongated sun-dappled woodland, to emerge at a wire fence, where the waymarked corner points to a marked gate ahead. From here the more open way ascends, on the same bearing, to yet another marked gate opening on to an extensive area of rough upland grazing. Ahead the fellside beckons; High Cap, the rippled gully of Ardale, and the sweeping ridges of Muska Hill and Brown Hill will all be enjoyed as the walk progresses.

Cross the rush-ridden land in a straight line north-east for approximately 500yds/m, making for Ardale Gully. As it draws closer a muddy cart track is joined to descend steeply into a meltwater channel below.

As the great ice cap blanketing East Fellside slowly began to melt, channels were gouged into the softer ground below by flows of melting ice. Many of these meltwater

*channels can be seen along East Fellside, snaking between
the rounded glaciated mounds of harder rock.*

Walls, gates and sheep pens lie ahead (at GR652343),
to be negotiated on the return journey. Turn left
before the gate for a few yards, to cross Ardale Beck
by a wide wooden platform, passing through the wall
via a small gate. Here a good track winds west with
the bracken-clad slopes to a large lime kiln (GR647344).

*In this substantial, well-preserved lime kiln, two arched
fire places can be seen, each sub-divided into three, giving
six hearths in all. Fed from above with limestone quarried
from the fells around Man at Edge, and brought down by
wagons on the tracked incline, the resultant high alka-
line lime was used to reduce the high acidity of the fell
pastures.*

Now begins a continuous ascent of 1,378ft/420m over
the next 3 miles/4.8km. At the track junction by the
kiln, turn right on to a winding grass way, ascending
north then north-east, alongside or on the wagonway
as it rises to the ruins of Man at Edge below Brown
Hill. Pass through a rickety gate, by the corner of the
building, to ascend north on a grass path to the col
between the dome of Muska Hill, left, and Brown Hill,
right. This short section, on a clear day, provides a
complete canvas over the Vale of Eden to the Lakeland
fells.

Once over the col, the way narrows and swings
slightly right, before descending to join a pathway
coming in from Muska Hill. Pass through a gate ahead.
By now the outliers, most with tiaras of limestone
scars, and Melmerby Fell ringed by Melmerby High
Scar, can be seen to the north, as can the line of our
route to Stony Rigg. First go through another gated
wall, then ascend over rough ground (beware sink

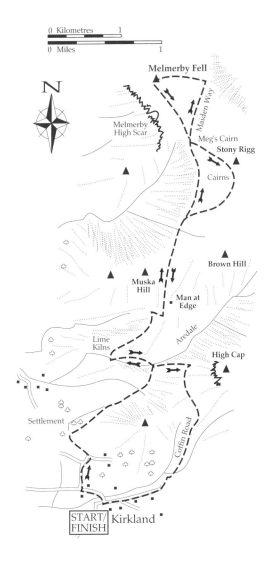

0 Kilometres 1
0 Miles 1

N

Melmerby Fell

Maiden Way

Melmerby
High Scar

Meg's Cairn

Stony Rigg

Cairns

Brown Hill

Muska
Hill

**Man at
Edge**

Aredale

Lime
Kilns

High Cap

Settlement

Coffin Road

START/
FINISH   Kirkland

holes) to a final gate, before rising to the many-cairned boulderfield topped by Meg's Cairn. The final strides to this large and somewhat untidy cone of stones is by a jinking track that avoids the worst of the boulders.

Maiden Way is a high-level Roman road, mentioned in 1179 in a church document and later in Camden's Britannica of 1586, from "Mayden Castle" by Stainmore to Hadrian's Wall. A well-supported theory suggests it was there to protect and transport lead, just as Hadrian's Wall was there, not to keep the Scots out, but to keep the Roman lead in. There were few lead deposits north of the Wall.

An upright, unmarked stone indicates a paved stretch of the Maiden Way as it contours north. Follow this, standard 7ft/2m wide Roman road for 300yds/m, before ascending west over the open flanks of Melmerby Fell (2,310ft/704m), to the small stone pile on its flat and grassy top.Return south-east, over trackless slopes, to Meg's Cairn.

For those wishing to vary the route of ascent, a thin trod leads south-south-east through the boulders of Stony Rigg, by a line of prominent cairns (not piles of stones). At the fourth cairn swing right to the wall, by two more cairns, and pass through a small gate. Here a twin track covers the fell south-west, to the ascent route prior to Muska and Brown Hill col.

For those not in favour of boulder-hopping, return to GR652343, east of the large lime kiln, and pass through the two gates by the sheep pens to zigzag east. Ascend with a cart track for 800yds/m to join the coffin road below the escarpment of High Cap. This section allows an intimate insight into the gaping jaws of Ardale, before turning right on to the wide and winding track for the final walled and fenced 1½ miles/2.4km to Kirkland Hall and Kirkland.

SOUTH TYNEDALE
AND NENTDALE

"Large rubbish heaps along the hillside show,
The vast extent of hollow ground below."
                    (Richard Watson)

"The Tyne, the Tyne, the coaly Tyne", although the coal
prefix is no longer true, the Tyne is the great river of the
North East, formed by the coming together of two rivers of
character, the North Tyne and the South Tyne.

The North Tyne flows from the flanks of Peel Fell in the
Cheviot range, while the South Tyne trickles to life on the
western skirts of Tynehead Fell, a river that burbles, booms
and flows through South Tynedale for some 45 miles/72km,
north and east, to Hexham, in the wide and fertile acres of
Tynedale.

Nentdale is a small tributary of South Tynedale, the two
joining at Alston, England's highest market town.

This section devotes its attention to the upper reaches of
South Tynedale, from Kirkhaugh, 3 miles/4.8km north of
Alston, to the head of both South Tynedale and Nentdale.
Both are narrow dales, their valley floors carpeted by green
and flowering pastures, bound in by miles of grey stone
walls, and surrounded by steep-sided fells and bleak, dark
moorland. The whole bears pockmarks and scars from the
hands of miner and quarryman.

The area was originally farmed, after the fashion of the
early Norse settlers, with herds of cattle and sheep, ascend-
ing and descending with the seasons. It was not until the
early 1800s and the advent of the Enclosure Acts, that the

two dales were enclosed. This was a period that also saw an improvement in the roads and tracks, helped greatly by the London Lead Company, the main mining employer in the two dales. Previously, lead ore had been carried over the open fell by teams of packhorses, known locally as "galloways", a method that often ground to a halt in the deep snows of a protracted Pennine winter.

Walkers, and the wheel, have benefited from the high contouring mine roads. Tracks, such as the lead road from Garrigill to Dufton (rising to 2,477ft/755m, below the summit of Great Dun Fell), and many of today's highways linking the dales, are overlaid on the old mine roads.

Main access roads, like the A689 from Nenthead to Weardale (rising to 2,056ft/627m at Killhope Cross), the B6277 Alston to Teesdale road, (touching 1,950ft/594m), all have the same idea. Other access roads into the two dales are the A686 from either Hexham or Penrith and the A689 from Carlisle and Brampton.

Walking in South Tynedale and Nentdale is a delight when the air is clear, for not only are the northern Pennines fully revealed, but also the Lakeland fells and the Northumbrian hills.

38 Alston and Whitley Castle

Constantly changing scenes and moods make this investigation of the South Tyne valley an exciting prospect. A quiet way, with the North Pennine countryside – the Romans liked it here – for company.

Distance:
6¾ miles/10.8km

Height gain:
673ft/205m

Walking time:
3½ hours

Start/Finish:
Alston. GR718465: above the River South Tyne at the meeting of the A686 Hexham-Lakeland road, the A689 Carlisle-Weardale road and the B6277 Teesdale road.

Type of walk:
Circular, scenic, moderately challenging, the way traverses a variety of public paths and bridleways, wooded tracks, pasture paths, cart tracks, fellside trods and quiet lanes.

Free parking in the market place and the railway station car park. Information centre and toilets.

Alston, at 984ft/300m England's highest market town, has many facilities for the walker and as such provides a good base for local walks.

From the railway station, walk north through the car park on to a prepared path between riverside silver birch and fenced narrow-gauge railtrack. Pass the repair shops and ageing engines and, at a swing gate, cross the track, right (east), and rise with the lane to a signpost ("Paddy's Well Steps"), pointing north.

Trains, hauled by steam and diesel, once more travel the old Alston-Haltwhistle branch line, albeit only as far as Gilderdale. The original line was opened in 1852 by the Newcastle & Carlisle Railway Company, and closed in 1976 by British Rail. (Tickets are available from Alston Station.)

Turn left with a hard-core track as far as a cottage. Beyond, a grassy way leads via riverside gate, stile and stone wall, to what appears to be a dead end, funnelled through encroaching woodland. There is, however, a stone stile in the right-hand wall leading on to an ascending and stepped path, through a bank of trees, to Paddy's Well Steps and a tree-lined lane. Swing left with the lane to clear the conifers and descend north-west to Randalholme Tower and Bridge, a gentle valley stretch of munching cattle and scuttling pheasants.

Randalholme is a defensive medieval pele tower, built to repel both reiving Border Scots and the wild men of Redesdale and the Debatable Land.

Cross Ayle Burn by Randalholme Bridge and, as the lane rises, a woodland track ascends right (north) into Kirkside Wood. It is a somewhat steep, but open track, that allows sightings of the Roman fort at Whitley Castle and the three curricks of Little Heaplaw to the west. After 800yds/m, break out of the trees into waymarked pastures, and swing left with arrowhead

waymarks to descend to the low lane at Underthank Farm.

Turn sharp right on to the lane, passing the tall-towered Kirkhaugh Church, before swinging left on a stiled way to cross the now visible Kirkhaugh footbridge spanning the South Tyne. Once over, it is sharp right with the riverbank, and then left at the gate, to follow a winding cart track that passes below the disused railbed at Kirkhaugh.

Haugh, a Norse word meaning "flat fertile land alongside a river", indicates the presence of Scandinavian settlers centuries ago.

At Kirkhaugh Farm turn left (south) with the waymarked Pennine Way for the return to Alston, a route that is mainly through walled pastures, passing Dyke House Farm on its east side prior to crossing the A689, and rising to the encircling embankments of Whitley Castle.

Whitley Castle, whose ridges and ditches are similar in size and design to those of the Vallum in Hadrian's Wall, is the only Roman fort within the area of the North Pennines. It is assumed that the Roman road – the Maiden Way – passed close by, and many support the theory that the Maiden Way and Whitley Castle were connected to the Romans' quest for lead and silver on Alston Moor. It is also likely that the domed Little Heaplaw, with its three curricks, was a link in the Roman chain of signal stations.

Continue south, over the deep cleugh of Gilderdale Burn, by waymarked footbridge, to rise and then descend east, crossing the A689 at Harbutlaw, circa 1870. By lane, pasture and narrow snicket the PW descends south past Harbut Lodge, eventually to emerge on a Tarmac lane at the old Alston brewery by the riverside. Cross the bridge and ascend left to explore the cobbled lanes and alleys of this interesting town.

39 Alston and Bleagate

A walk that delights the eye, pleases the ear and is never severe on limbs and lungs. Wild flowers abound, as do the riverside and woodland birds, their spring and summer song blending with the music of the shingled South Tyne. The walk passes through the agricultural past, and present, of South Tynedale.

Distance:
4 miles/6.4km

Height gain:
148ft/45m

Walking time:
2-3 hours

Start/Finish:
Alston. GR718465: easily reached from Hexham, Brampton, the Vale of Eden, Teesdale, Weardale and Allendale.

Type of walk:
A pastoral circuit, with many stiles, that is accomplished with ease. Public paths through pastures, including a stretch of the Pennine Way, quiet country lanes and green cart tracks depart and return to Alston.

Free parking at the railway station car park and in the market place.

Alston, whose streets are narrow and steep, furnishes all that is required of a good walk's start and finish. From the railway station, or the market cross, walk south through the town with the A686 to the South Tyne. Prior to the bridge, swing left with the YHA sign, then right on to a tree-lined waymarked path south.

"Alston town is a small market town, meanly built, situated in a declivity of a steep hill, inhabited by miners. Pent in a narrow valley over which mountains frowned with a melancholy sterility and nakedness." (W Hutchinson, 1785-1794.)

The same gentleman also recorded, "Aldston Moor, where all that the earth produces is from its bowels, where the people are also subterraneous."

Continue through this amazing mix of conifers to emerge on to a continuous series of walled pastures, either alongside or above the tinkling shingle of the River South Tyne.

Gap stiles, stepped stiles and mini-gated stiles funnel the pasture path south, by the footbridge, over the innocuous trickle of Nattrass Gill – look out for a different Nattrass Gill on the return route. After 1¼ miles/ 2km of this green and pleasant path, on the old route to Garrigill, the buildings of Bleagate Farm are reached. Pass through the yard by a waymarked stile, to leave the Pennine Way by swinging left (north-east), up the narrow lane.

Bleagate, the word can be traced back to the 1200s, is recorded as meaning a "grazing for 'nolte' or 'kine' (cattle)".

A gentle ascent by Scarberry Hill, where the way takes the left fork to travel north on a wind-whistling way, by a conifer plantation, to Woodstock House and the driveway to High Nest. At the sheep pens, as the lane turns sharp right, swing left into High Nest's drive for a few strides, then cross the wall right by a

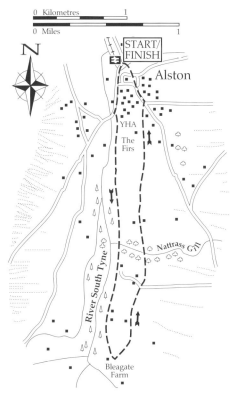

waymarked stone stile leading through a damp and rushy pasture. Continue north, skirting the golf hole, to enter the woods by yet another waymarked stile and descend sharply to the footbridge directly over High Nest Falls. Steps lead out of Nattrass Gill and the way north drops to the old stones of Annat Walls Farm, from where a lane covers the last mile/1.6km to the old almshouses and Alston.

40 Ashgill Force

This short walk through "Gerard's Glen" provides constant interest for all: an abundance of wildlife, the spectacular falls of Ashgill, the small, steep-sided gorge of the South Tyne and constant reminders of its lead mining past. Never severe, the circuit is always rewarding, a colourful low level interlude in a wilderness of endless fells.

Distance:
4 1/2 miles/7.2km

Height gain:
262ft/80m

Walking time:
3 hours

Start/Finish:
Garrigill. GR745415: on the River South Tyne, 3 miles/4.8km south-south-east of Alston, and 3 1/4 miles/ 5.2km west from Nenthead.

Type of walk:
A circular pastoral and waterside ramble of rare beauty. Underfoot, waymarked lanes, many stiled pasture paths and stepped riverside ways, which can be slippery in places after rain.

Limited parking in the village, requiring care and consideration.

Garrigill was once a noisy mining centre, but now it is a tranquil delight in the summer's sun and a haven in winter's blow. Its name derives from Gerard, a Saxon, who is thought to have grazed his stock on the summer pastures of South Tynedale, was from Roman times a lead mining hamlet. Indeed, enough silver was extracted to warrant a Royal Mint in Carlisle, and the lead also was much prized. Clairvaux Abbey in France and Windsor Castle were both roofed with South Tynedale lead.

From the village green walk south, between the church and the many-windowed Ivy House Farm, passing the old Fox Inn beyond the churchyard, to reach the Black Band miners' track and the Pennine Way swinging right. Continue south with the Tarmac lane.

Ivy House was home to Westgarth Forster, a renowned geologist who died in poverty. The church was founded in 1215, but the present building dates from the late 1700s and has had its share of hard times; coal for the church stove used to be kept in the pews. The old Fox Inn, two buildings beyond the churchyard, was much favoured by Liberals, miners and poachers. So successful were the poachers that local estates hired the services of a troop of cavalry, recently returned from the Napoleonic Wars, to halt the loss of game. Local knowledge prevailed and the miners/poachers led the soldiers a merry dance before disappearing into one of the nearby mines.

After approximately 500yds/m along this quiet country lane, the tidy steading and tree-sheltered house of Low Crossgill is reached on the right. Leave the road, left, at the gate (signposted "Ashgill"), to walk with the narrow lonnen to Windshaw Bridge. Pause on this bridge to admire the water-worn rocks and the hurrying South Tyne before turning right to continue south along the waymarked east river bank. Here begins one of the most delightful stretches in

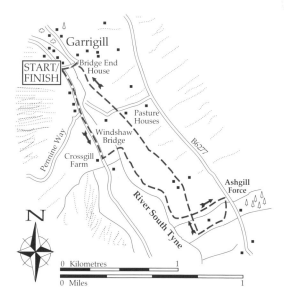

the North Pennines, a wonderland of nature's treasures.

At the confluence of Tyne and Ash Gills, leave the woodside path to turn left (east), with the gill over a terraced pasture, to a four-way direction post by a footbridge over Ash Gill – the return route. Continue east, by stile and kissing gate, into a fissured dene of many waterfalls, climaxing with the bridge-framed Ashgill Force. Prepared paths, stone steps and footbridges lead through the flower and tree-lined gully to the streaming cascade of Ash Gill below the arched road bridge, circa 1920, that replaced its collapsed predecessor. In the grip of winter, a frozen Ashgill Force is a visual delight.

As the fall is approached, note the arched entrance to Ashgill Horse Level, a drift or tunnel that ran to the Wellhope Knot Vein, a rich vein of galena, worked in the early 1800s. Horse-drawn wagons carried the ore to the surface via the arched entrance of the level, built to a certain shape and size to allow the mine ponies easy passage.

Return as if to the lower footbridge. Before it is reached ascend left on a grassy path above the storage bays and through the trees, to a stile and Bird's Nest, the much-used name for Waterfall Cottage. The cottage has a colourful past, having been a blacksmith's shop and later a Primitive Methodist meeting place and Sunday school.

Once through the gate the path descends, then swings right to cross Ash Gill by the footbridge met on the outward journey. With the crosspath fingerpost ("Garrigill"), rise sharply north by path and pasture wall to the collection of cottages known as Ashgillside. These are passed by means of six waymarked stiles, to begin a pleasing and scenic return north on a stiled waymarked way. First to Pasture Houses, with fine views to Garrigill and over South Tynedale, then to a lonely steading at Snappergill, leaving left via the waymarked field gate to descend diagonally to the far corner of the pasture. One more narrow stile, foot-bridge and gate lead by the woodside to the white cottages of Bridge End House and the high bridge (circa 1891) over the South Tyne. On the return to the village green and the old stepped forge, the restored village hall and the George and Dragon Inn are passed.

In the days when poachers were pursued by the cavalry, thriving Garrigill's population was in excess of 1,600; today it has evaporated to a mere 220.

41 Tyne Head and Trout Beck

The daleheads of Tees, Wear and South Tyne provide a dramatic backdrop for this stimulating journey, accompanied by the signs of the past and the sounds of the present. An adventure providing far-reaching views and much satisfaction. Waymarks are few; not so the many natural navigational aids such as becks, hushes, cairns and stone walls. Be prepared on this high fell walk for changing conditions.

Distance:
13 miles/20.9km

Height gain:
1,296ft/395m

Walking time:
7 hours

Start: *GR758384: a cart track fork 250yds/m south of Hill House Farm, at the southern end of the lane, 2¹/₂ miles/4km south from Garrigill.*

Finish: *Milburn. GR656293.*

Type of walk:
A demanding linear walk, traversing the dalehead watershed. The way is by miners' track, narrow fell paths, Tarmac and dirt lanes, trackless fell and pasture paths.

There is very limited parking either at the start or finish, so take care not to block field, road or household access.

The higher reaches of upper South Tynedale, layered by sandstone, shale and limestone, provide the starting gate for this high level walk. Walk south along the right fork, with the Tarmac and, later, hard-core public bridleway, passing Noonstones Hill on the right before Dorthgill is reached. To the left, the green gouge of Clargill Burn containing the old hamlet of Tynehead, is prominent.

Noonstone is in the local Domesday Book, the 14th-century Black Book of Hexham, as a Norse settlement. Dorthgill, a miner's/farmer's house known as Tea Kettle Hall, stands surrounded by old mines. Tynehead was close to the Clargill Vein, the richest silver producer in the North Pennines, yielding up to 40oz of silver per ton of lead.

Continue south with the descending track, below Cocklake Mine, to reach and cross the glinting crystal-lined waters of the South Tyne by a 20th-century barn and the remains of an 18th-century smelt mill.

A small waterfall tumbles over the Whin Sill where the flower-lined way, including thyme, mountain pansy, yarrow and Grass of Parnassus, was once trodden by Scottish drovers and their black highland cattle.

As the snow-poled way ascends with the dwindling South Tyne, below yesterday's mines of Calvert, Tynebogs and Dosey, it passes the remains of what were the highest inhabited dwellings in England. A clutch of trickles ooze in from the left, before the Tyne-Tees watershed – such is the rather disappointing source of the Tyne. Compensation is provided by the triple tops of Great and Little Dun Fell and Cross Fell to the west. The steady descent south-east continues to heaps of sterile spoil and broken mine shops at Troutbeck Foot.

Swing right at the fork and cross, via a vehicular bridge, the surprisingly wide Tees to join the northern bank of Trout Beck, a constant companion southwest for the next 3½ miles/5.2km. Soon, on the left, just beyond the bridge and gate to Moor House, Trout Beck displays a delightful series of small, stepped cascades.

Moor House, a former shooting lodge, is now a national nature reserve and England's leading research site into global warming and the natural environment. It is managed by English Nature.

The route alongside Trout Beck, to the "golf ball" on Great Dun Fell, is initially on a dirt and stony track that eventually tapers to a narrow trod as it ascends. Several times it crosses the beck, but never wanders far from its banks, showing in places the bed of the old mine road from Knock. Ascent to the conspicuous hush of Dun Fell, the riven, lead-poisoned sides of the fell devoid of vegetation, is never severe, and aided by a definitive way and the occasional marker post and pile of stones.

Constant summer companions over this wilderness of blanket-bog and peat are burnside dippers and ring ouzels, and on the fells golden plover, snipe, curlew and chattering red grouse.

To the right, fractionally below Dunfell Hush, is the smaller Henrake Hush. Dunfell Hush is ascended, either by a path up its narrow floor or on a cinder track along its southern rim, to meet the waymarked Pennine Way as it clips its western extremity.

Hushing, the scouring of hillsides by vast quantities of water to expose the underlying lead veins, was forbidden by Act of Parliament in the early 1800s, an Act no doubt

ignored by T'Aud Man. The geodesic dome and associated devices are to aid the Civil Aviation Authority.

Follow the peat path of the Pennine Way left (south), to join the Tarmac and snow poles of the access road. As the road swings right, stay with it to descend beneath the castellated limestone escarpment of Green Castle towering above on the right.

At the foot of this dominating gorge turn right on to a wide dirt road, contouring north-west for 1¼ miles/ 2km to the modern-day barytes mine at Silver Band. Between a small spoil heap on the left and a man-made

made pond ahead, a small gap leads left to a cairn some 100yds/m south-west. From this point, for the next mile/1.6km, over a grass and boulder-strewn shelved fell, there is no clear path. Although shown on the map as a public bridleway, the route is assisted only by a few piles of marker stones.

From the cairn by the mine, cross the fell south-west to a small but definite pile of stones on an escarpment rim. Descend south-west via a grassy gap, by scattered boulders, to a large cairn on the next level.

Navigation is aided by keeping a line of collapsed gantries, from an old aerial-way, always to the left. Yet another grassy gap aids passage down the stony slope, to a further plateau with a large cairn ahead, to the south-west. At this cairn, do not attempt to descend the steep boulder-strewn escarpment. Note the gated wall below, with incoming paths, then trek either left or right along the rim for 100yds/m or so, before descending diagonally to the field gate.

Now with pastures green, and guiding walls on the left, plus views of Wildboar Scar and Cross Fell on the right, descend at ease, first west then south-west for 2¹/₂ miles/4km to the fellside hamlet of Milburn. It is waymarked for the final 1³/₄ miles/2.8km.

Milburn, as with so many of the fellside villages, is built around a pleasant green, and in the past housed those employed in the mines and in agriculture.

42 Nent and Loaning Head

Constantly changing scenes are a delight on this walk, as are the varying flowers, grasses and varied species of moorland and waterside birds. Even stark reminders of the lead mining past can provide many intriguing interludes, not least in witnessing nature's efforts to restore the status quo. Numerous waymarks and natural features along the way serve to aid navigation.

Distance:
9½ miles/15.25km

Height gain:
1,083ft/330m

Walking time:
5-5½ hours

Start/Finish:
Nenthead. GR781436: a custom-built lead mining village on the A689; 5¾ miles/9.2km north-west from Cowshill, Weardale, and 5 miles/8km south-east of Alston.

Type of walk:
A typical daleshead circular walk over mine tracks, open fells, pastoral and waterside paths, and forest lanes. Although demanding at times and wet in places, it is nevertheless a rewarding journey.

Free central parking and toilets.

Nenthead, or "Nent", to use its dales name, is proud to be England's highest village (1,530ft/466m), and to have the highest church above sea-level. For the hill walker Nent provides a perfect start.

From the car park, with its information board, walk left (south-west), to the white-washed hamlet of Overwater; turning, first left, into a cobbled lane leading to a stile and signpost (Fiddler Street).

Nenthead, as it is today, did not exist before the 1700s, although Picts and, later, Romans were thought to have lived and possibly worked the mines around Alston Moor.

In the 1750s, the London Lead Company, known also as the Quaker Company, acquired the majority of the Nent valley mining leases. The company, a considerate employer, developed the custom-built village of Nenthead for miners, officials and their families. It included a school, chapel, piped water, post office, shops, inn, public library, plus public washhouse and baths. Note also the memorial drinking fountain, twin to the one in Middleton-in-Teesdale, and dedicated to Robert Bainbridge, superintendent to the company. More detailed information is available at the heritage centre and the post office.

The way ascends south-west by Dowgang Burn, with wall and wood, for 500yds/m. At a table-like earthfast rock beneath a tall larch, cross the stiled wall to leave this hushed gully west over a pasture, and cross the Nenthead-Garrigill road into Fiddler Street. A sign ("King's Head Cottages") points north, along a stone-paved path by crumbling cottages, with a bird's-eye view of Nentdale. At the fourth abandoned dwelling, circle the building ascending west over spoil heaps into walled rush-ridden pastures, containing many of the 300 moorland plants that grow in the area. Posts and stiles lead to the corner of a sitka plantation, where

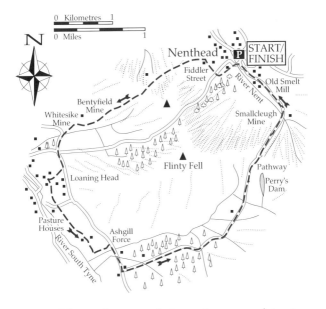

a squelchy perimeter path turns the corner, later to leave the trees for a drier waymarked south-west route above Greengill Hush.

Surrounded by the sombre mine-scarred fells of Black Moss and Nunnery Hill, the path descends to a finger of trees cloaking the steep sides of the infant Garrigill Burn. Pass by the north side of the wind-blown pines, past a standing stone, to a signpost and stone steps in the cleugh below. Swing right (west), on a grass track, by the rusty waters of the narrow gully, to wind by the ruins of Bentyfield Mine and then, at lower levels, the Whitesike Mine.

Bentyfield and Whitesike provide fine examples of the North Pennines' industrial heritage. Please take great care in the vicinity of these old workings, although one shaft at Whitesike, protected by a dome of stone with a metal grill, allows closer examination.

Whitesike opens on to the B6277, Alston-Teesdale road. Swing left for 500yds/m of roadside scenic walking, crossing the Nenthead-Garrigill road.

Far-ranging views ahead reveal the ski tows on Yad Moss, below Burnhope Seat and Herdship Fell.

At the Loaning Head sign turn right, descending steeply to the tidy houses, then follow the public path to Pasture Houses, turning left for a gentle pastoral South Tyne valley stroll above Garrigill.

A series of stiles and strategically-placed waymarks map the route by Windy Hall and Pasture Houses to Ashgillside, an assembly of former smallholders' cottages, negotiated by six stiles. Beyond, the path drops to the tumbling waters of Ash Gill.

Turn left (east), at the four-way signpost, through a wooded dene passing several exquisite stepped cascades to the bridge-framed wonder of Ashgill Force.

Ashgill Force, perhaps the finest and most secluded waterfall in England, allows careful passage behind its streaming veil, a place much-favoured by dancing fairies, and ring ouzels.

Leave the dene by retracing the path towards the footbridge, but prior to the bridge ascend left with a steep, stepped path to Ashgill Farm, by the road and bridge above Ashgill Force. Turn right along the B6277 for 250yds/m to Mid Ashgill cottage, and enter, left, the extensive coniferous plantations of Ashgill Wood. A measured ascent east, along what is now the Alternative Pennine Way, crossing Grue Gill and later Little Gill, eventually breaks the forest's grip by Hunter's Cleugh. Below, the narrowing gully of Ash Gill and ahead, the isolated hill farm of Priorsdale, surrounded by wind-swept fells, guide the way north-east, by a stony track, to the trident junction by Perry's Dam.

Perry's Dam, built 1847, held eight million gallons of water, providing a constant supply to power waterwheels and dressing plants.

Continue with the now wide and stony quarry track, to the pass leading down to the rock-strewn defile that is Nentdale Head. This ravine of dark shadows, with a concentration of the paraphernalia of lead and mineral mining, cannot be matched in the North Pennines. Keep to your chosen path, winding by crumbling mining debris, to the cast-doune Nenthead Smelt Mill, an area of sterile, yet appealing, desolation that is left via a metal gate at Mill Cottage. The short return to the car park passes the heritage centre (scheduled to open in 1996), and over the Nent to the arched entrance of Dowgang Level.

Nenthead Smelt Mill, mid-1700s to 1890s, now chimneyless, also contained an assay house and laboratory. Close by is the long building, nicknamed the Barracks, that housed the foreign workers employed by the Vieille Montagne Zinc Company of Belgium.

The heritage centre occupies the site of the company sawmill, a mill that prepared the company-grown timber for use in the mines and the village. More than 250 hectares/ 550 acres of larch and pine were planted, often at heights up to 2,000ft/600m, far higher than is considered practical today.

43 Nent and Wellhope Moor

Although not long, this ridge-top route packs a challenge to legs and lungs, revealing much that is good, and a little of what was not so good, in this heartland of the upper dales. For maximum enjoyment choose a clear, far-seeing day. Nenthead itself will also repay a visit.

Distance:
6½ miles/10.4km

Height gain:
761ft/232m

Walking time:
3½ hours

Start/Finish:
Nenthead. GR781436: a one-time model mining village on the A689; 5 miles/8km south-east from Alston, and 5¾ miles/9.2km west-north-west of Cowshill.

Type of walk:
A moderate, two counties circuit from valley floor to moorland top, walking along village lanes, farm tracks, miners' ways and open fell: a bracing journey, with the wind and the birds for company.

Central parking prior to the heritage centre.

Nenthead, known simply as Nent, is a North Pennine Mecca for both walking and lead mining aficionados.

Walk north, with the Alston road, from the Miner's Arms, and opposite Wright Brothers' garage – former Rampgill Smelt Mill for the processing of zinc and lead – swing right at the public footpath sign ("Gudham Gill & Wellgill") on to a narrow lane running with Hillersdon Terrace. Continue north on this straight way to leave the houses.

Nenthead began to grow in the mid-1700s, when the London Lead Company embarked on an expansion of mills, mines and, in the early 1800s, a model village for their employees. Hillersdon Terrace was one of the many rows of houses and cottages built, housing at the Miner's Arms end the mill agent, the surgeon and the schoolmaster. Next were smelters – a craftsmen's trade, and overmen – foremen or overseers, initially at rents of £4 to £6 per annum. Schools, social benefits and health care were all contributed to by the socially-aware Quaker Company.

Continue north past a Northumbrian Water installation, surrounded by lanes leading to Wellgill Farm above. At the next fork swing left and hop over a small stile on to a narrow path running north with the restructured and reinforced river bank. Cross Gudham Gill by a footbridge bearing the notice "This is not a dedicated right of way, but the County Council as landowner is willing to commit its use on foot only."

Once over, bear right past an arched and sealed adit, the remains of mine buildings, to meet two directional markers. Follow the left one, ("Nenthall Valley View") rising via a stile, on grass and stone, past a converted cottage to the roadway ahead.

Swing left (north-west), to stride by Rock House (1642), and the tree-sheltered mansion of Greenends. Ignore the signpost opposite Greenends and continue with the road for a further 400yds/m before turning right, via a field gate ("Public Footpath: Carrshield") to ascend north with a winding stone and grass mine track. It is a scenic zigzag route, distinct and frequently gated and waymarked, that rises to the walled boundary of Cumbria and Northumberland at Hunter's Break, with the heather-clad hump of Whimsey Hill to the right.

Did the name originate from the 17th-century "whimseys" used in raising lead ore by horse-power? Two to four horses circled around a large drum, securely anchored, winding mine ropes with buckets of ore attached.

Descend over Wellhope Moor to the conspicuous rusting and rotting remains of Wellhope Shaft. All around the wilderness prevails: endless folds of heather, rush, matgrass and molinia-clad fells, home to curlew, snipe, dunlin, golden plover and grouse.

Wellhope Shaft, 416ft/127m deep, was sunk in 1925 by the Belgian Vieille Montagne Zinc Company. This shaft connected with Haggs Mine, a level that entered the daleside below Nentsberry, 1¼ miles/2km south-west and 460ft/ 140m below Wellhope Moor. An aerial flight by a series of gantries and suspended buckets took the "bouse" (lead and minerals from the veins) to be sorted and smelted at New Mill, Nenthead. Gantries can still be seen on Wellhope Moor. USE EXTREME CAUTION IN THE VICINITY OF MINES AND SHAFTS.

Leave behind the mine shop and heaps of "gangue" – the miners' name for unwanted discards – as blue arrowheads direct east over a narrow grass-covered grooved way, descending to the remains of Wellhopehead Lead Mine at a meeting of sikes with Wellhope Burn. Over the rocky confluence a stepped way assists passage before ascending east-north-east,

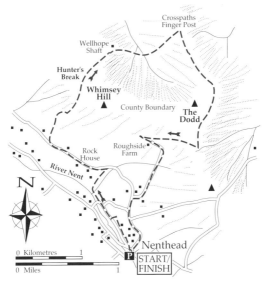

with more markers, past a rectangular sheepfold to meet a crosspath signpost on the ridge ahead.

Turn right (south-east) and then south at this four-fingered post, to stride out with some style on a clearway contouring The Dodd and Dodd's End, to reach the county boundary wall once more. At the waymarked gate turn right into Cumbria, and follow the half-hidden track west to the isolated and abandoned stones of Roughside Farm. From here a wide, and in places rutted, track descends east and south to Dykeheads Farm. To the south the trees and chimneyed roofs of Nent can be seen, and easily reached, by following the lane left from Dykeheads by Whitehall to the cobbled lanes and washed cottages of the oldest part of the village, Gillgill Lane and journey's end.

Useful Information

YOUTH HOSTELS
Baldersdale: Blackton, Barnard Castle, DL12 9UP
(01833) 650629
Dufton: Redstones, Dufton, Appleby, CA16 6DB
(01768) 351236
Langdon Beck: Forest-in-Teesdale, Barnard Castle
DL12 0XN (01833) 622228
Alston: The Firs, Alston, Cumbria, CA9 3RW
(01434) 381509
Edmundbyers: Low House, Edmundbyers, Consett,
DH8 9NL (01207) 670143
Ninebanks: Orchard House, Mohope, Hexham,
NE47 8DO (01434) 345288
Greenhead: Greenhead, Carlisle, CA6 7HG
(01697) 735798
Once Brewed: Military Road, Bardon Mill, Hexham,
NE47 7AN (01434) 344360

CAMPING BARNS
(Bookings: YHA Northern Region, PO Box 11,
Matlock, Derbyshire (01629) 825850. 24hr
answerphone.)
Blackcleugh Farm: Wearhead
Long Way Farm: Holwick
Witton Castle Estate: Witton le Wear
Pecknell Farm: Lartington

TOURIST INFORMATION CENTRES
Alston: Railway Station (01434) 381696
Appleby-in-Westmorland: Moot Hall (01768) 351177
Barnard Castle: Galgate (01833) 690909
Brampton: Moot Hall (01697) 73433
Hexham: Hallgates (01434) 605225
Kirkby Stephen: (017683) 71199
Stanhope: Dales Centre (01833) 527650

HERITAGE AND VISITOR CENTRES
Allenheads Heritage Centre: Allenheads
(01434) 685395
Killhope Wheel Lead Mining Centre: Killhope
(01388) 537505
Bowlees Visitor Centre: Bowlees (01388) 62292
Hamsterley Forest Visitor Centre: Hamsterley
(01388) 488312
Northumbrian Water Visitor Centre: Grassholme
(01833) 650204/640344

MISCELLANEOUS
Bowes Museum: Barnard Castle (01833) 690606
East Cumbria Countryside Project: Carlisle
(01228) 561160
North Pennines Tourism Partnership: Alston
(01434) 382069
Northumbrian Water: Pity Me, Durham, DH1 5FJ
(0191) 383 2222
RSPB Geltsdale Reserve (01228) 70205
Talkin Tarn Country Park: Brampton (01697) 73129
Warcop Training Range: Warcop (01768) 341661
Weardale Museum of High House Chapel:
Ireshopeburn (01388) 537417

Cover photo: High Cup Nick
(John Cleare/Mountain Photography)

Printed by Hubbard Print, Dronfield, near Sheffield

Acknowledgements

To those who willingly gave of their time and their knowledge to a stranger, my thanks and appreciation to all. In particular to Keith Watson, Robert Walton of Blackcleugh Farm, Chris Pringle and Dave Higgs of Northumbrian Water, Simon Blenkinsop of Forest Enterprise and Mike Wenham of Ninebanks YH, for their shared expertise. I am also indebted to the Wolsingham branch of Durham County Library Service, whose smiling co-operation provided many insights into the North Pennines and their lead mining past. Last but not least, my thanks to the regular team of advisers on matters grammatical and photographic, and also to those well-met along the way.

This book has been compiled in accordance with the Guidelines for Writers of Path Guides published by the Outdoor Writers' Guild.

By the same author
The Border Country: A Walker's Guide
Border Pubs and Inns
Kielder Country Walks

Index